THE
BIG
TIME

1817

**HARPER & ROW,
PUBLISHERS**
New York

*Cambridge, Philadelphia
San Francisco, London
Mexico City, São Paulo
Singapore, Sydney*

THE
BIG
TIME

The Harvard Business School's most success-ful class — and how it shaped America

Laurence Shames

Designed by Ruth Bornschlegel

Library of Congress Cataloging-in-Publication Data
Shames, Laurence.
    The big time.

    Includes index.
    1. Harvard University. Graduate School of Business Administration.
Class of 1949—Biography. 2. Harvard University. Graduate School of
Business   Administration—Alumni—Biography.   3.   Businessmen—
United States—Biography. I. Title.
HF1134.H4S5   1986   650′.07′117444   84-47598
ISBN 0-06-015278-8

86 87 88 89 90 RRD 10 9 8 7 6 5 4 3 2

*For my parents, for Elsie, and in memory
of Harry and of Arnold Albert*

contents

acknowledgments

I would like, first of all, to express my thanks to the men of the Harvard Business School Class of 1949, without whose candor, enthusiasm, and ripe capacity for self-examination this book would not have been possible. My especial gratitude is due to Ernest F. Henderson III, the Class Secretary; to Roger Sonnabend and James S. Craig, cochairmen of the Class's thirty-fifth reunion; and to Arnold Berlin, whose warm interest in the project has been a boon.

My appreciation also goes out to Harriet Rubin, Ed Burlingame, Sterling Lord, and Stuart Krichevsky for their support and their steadfastness in the clinches. I would like to express my thanks to Lawrence E. Joseph, who far outstripped his stated role of researcher to become an active partner in the book's conception. To Ed Wetschler, good friend and grand master of the telling historical detail, my very warmest appreciation. And to Jade Albert, my companion, a profound sigh of relief that we didn't wait till the book was done.

L.S.

. . . it was the age of wisdom, it was the age
of foolishness, it was the epoch of belief . . .
the season of Light . . . the spring of hope
. . . we had everything before us . . .

PART I

"The Class the Dollars Fell On"

one

That Rare and Golden Ticket

Maybe. They were telling him maybe.

He wasn't in, but he wasn't flat-out rejected either. He was on the wait list, he was dangling.

It was 1947. He'd been in the Navy for three years and out of the Navy for a couple of months, and here he was, standing in line again. What it came down to was that there were seven hundred or so guys that Harvard Business School thought better of, and if enough of them didn't show, he'd back into a berth. The next move was his. He could tell them forget it and spend his GI dollars elsewhere or he could sit tight and chew his nails like an ugly girl who maybe gets called for a Friday date on Thursday. It was humiliating.

It was also unprecedented. He, Stanley Greenfield, not make the cut? This was news. He'd been one of the brainiest kids in one of the brainiest schools in Brooklyn, a standout in a school of four thousand street-smart Depression brats who'd been taught that glowing report cards would lead straight on to success, to respect, to contentment itself. He'd taken all the right advice, had played the game with a passion. A high-school guidance counselor had once told Stanley that extracurricular activities looked good on your record, so Stanley ran everything from the chess club to the candy drive. Then, here at Johns Hopkins at either end of the war, he'd been business manager of the dramatics troupe, president of his fraternity, a founder of the National Student Association, and had muled his way, despite an impressive lack of natural talent, to varsity letters in track and soccer. Here was a kid as directed as gravity and well rounded as a bowling ball, a born operator, the cream of young American manhood, and Harvard Business School was telling him *maybe?*

Well, maybe wasn't good enough. Maybe gave Stanley Greenfield a rash. Of all the things you just couldn't expect a guy like him to do, sitting still and waiting topped the list. He was twenty-two, and in 1947 twenty-two was pretty old. You were supposed to know what you were doing by twenty-two. Greenfield read the notice three times, four times, then dropped it on his dormitory dresser and paced the room. He paced until his spirits had dug in, pivoted, and turned from abject misery to crazed enthusiasm. Suddenly he had a plan. More by reflex than decision, he found himself yanking the cardboard out of a fresh white shirt, then knotting a wide blue tie so tightly that his pulse slammed against his collar and he heard the ocean from the wrong side of his eardrums. He tried to brush his hair but it was at that half-grown-out stage, no longer standing up in a clean-cut military crew but not quite ready to lie down either. The hell with it—everybody's hair looked like that in the spring of '47; it was no disgrace. He grabbed a sport jacket, stuffed the notice into an inside pocket, and was out the door, heading for the next train from Baltimore to Boston.

Stanley Greenfield wore taps on his shoes back then. Over the years they'd saved him maybe fifteen bucks in worn-out soles and heels, plus they'd given a jaunty musicality to his steps, and now they ticked and scratched in the dormitory hallway as he ran. At a corner of the building he hit a long and scraping slide, scudding right past his roommate as he scratched on by.

"Hell you going?" the roommate asked.

"Harvard," said Stanley Greenfield, halfway down the next leg of hall by now.

"You got in?"

Greenfield looked over his shoulder and, taps ticking, shot back a grin that was as cocky as America in the spring of '47. "I will," he said. "I will."

In 1974, on the occasion of its twenty-fifth reunion, the Harvard Business School Class of 1949, the class that Stanley Greenfield had been scrambling to join, was dubbed, by *Fortune* magazine, "the class the dollars fell on."

In twelve glossy pages of near-idolatrous prose, Time Inc. was giving its immortalizing nod to a reputation that had been taking shape for a quarter of a century, that was already part of the folklore of boardrooms, clubhouses, and gatherings of alumni. The reputation, to put it simply, was this: that the Class of '49 had turned out to be the most wildly successful batch of MBAs to have shared a campus, anywhere, ever.

Pick your criterion—job titles, influence either official or *sub rosa*, or money pure and simple; by whatever measure, these guys were the hottest bunch ever to come down the chute. There were a mere 652 men in the Class of '49, yet everywhere you looked in the upper branches of American enterprise—in 1986 even more so than in '74—there they seemed to be. A '49er was sitting in the chairman's seat at Xerox; his former roommate was running Johnson & Johnson. A '49er had become the first man in history to buy a television network. A '49er was presiding over the biggest single chunk of General Dynamics, another was piloting Rohm & Haas, another occupied the chairmanship of Bloomingdale's. One '49er had his very own international conglomerate, named after himself. Forty-niners headed up utilities in the Northwest, hotel chains in New England, and investment firms smack in the heart of Wall Street. They held senior partnerships at Goldman, Sachs and at Booz, Allen and Hamilton, and filled crucial financial roles at American Standard and Morgan Guaranty. They were presidents of pension funds and presidents of colleges and presidents of companies that made lipstick and mascara. One '49er had been in Congress, another had run for governor of Mississippi, and another was in the hot seat as Ronald Reagan's chairman of the SEC. One Class member had parlayed a popcorn concession into ownership of a chain of movie theaters.

As of 1974, with the dollar worth roughly double what it would be a decade later, nearly one '49er in five had already become a millionaire. The Class's collective wealth, bolstered by a number of mammoth family fortunes, was hovering around the $2 billion mark. Forty-niners owned, on average, just a fraction under three homes apiece, had christened as many boats as comprised the Spanish Armada, and were piloted around in a fleet of private and corporate planes numbering nearly a hundred. Collectively, they held an estimated $460 million in securities. Forty-five percent of the men in the Class were either CEOs or chief operating officers of the companies that employed them. Collectively, those companies had annual revenues well in excess of $50 billion, employed over a million people, and held thirteen slots in *Fortune*'s directories of the nation's biggest concerns in manufacturing, banking, retailing, and financial service.

The class the dollars fell on. The moniker was a play on that of the West Point Class of 1915, Eisenhower's year, which had earned the nickname "the class the *stars* fell on." That group had shown an extraordinary knack for becoming generals—in large part because their careers were juiced up by two perfectly timed world wars. The '49ers' eminence, too, was conspired in by history—not by war directly, but by the longest, richest, and most widespread peacetime boom that the modern world had ever seen.

They could not have hit it better. In June of 1949, just as the Class was claiming its diplomas, the last of the tremulous postwar recessions was ending. The peacetime economy had finally found its legs and the big time in America was revving up in earnest. For nearly a quarter-century, economic growth would rocket forward virtually without a hitch. Fortunes would be made in everything from transistors to Everglades real estate to Wiffle balls, and statisticians would have to invent new words for the amounts of money changing hands. The men of '49, optimally placed and boundlessly ambitious, would both ride and guide that astonishing expansion, and in so doing would become emblematic of the swaggering influence of Harvard and of the mysterious potency of the MBA degree back when it was still exotic, a rare and golden ticket to the action. More than that, the men of '49 would become the standard-bearers of the bullish America that believed that Yank preeminence somehow stood outside of history, that breakneck growth could feed on itself forever, that scale would triumph and marketing moxie would always move the goods.

Theirs was the operative philosophy that would make America famously rich, and that, in the course of the very same euphoric decades, would encrust American enterprise with the sort of flaccid thinking, quaint stratagems, and wrong assumptions that even now are being slowly and painfully chipped away. Nothing is harder in the world than to change what used to be a winning game back when the game was simpler.

"We didn't ask to see you," said the Dean.

Stanley Greenfield nodded, shrugged, and tried to smile. He'd stopped running just long enough to get his shoes shined in South Station, and now, though he told himself he should be devoting 110 percent of his attention to the interview, he couldn't get it out of his mind to wonder if the Dean had noticed the fresh polish before they'd sat down on opposite sides of the desk and the gleaming leather was hidden by three feet of mahogany. A trivial thing, maybe, but things like that mattered. The dimple in the tie, the sliver of shirt cuff that showed beneath the jacket, the crisp crease in the pleat-front trousers—don't ask Stanley Greenfield where he'd picked up on those things, because he couldn't have said. It wasn't Flatbush, it wasn't the Pacific. But somehow, if you were a natural, you knew. And Harvard Business School was looking for the naturals—that much was clear, if circular. The Business School would make successes of the guys who didn't need the Business School to succeed.

The Dean had made his fingers into a steeple. He had a look on his face that might have been avuncular or might have been menacing—who could tell with these blithe academics, these guys who were set for life and whose job it was to decide who *else* would be? He rustled papers, stuffed his pipe, fumbled in numerous pockets for a match. Finally he said there was only one thing he wanted to ask Stanley Greenfield: why was it important enough to him to get into the B School so that he'd drop whatever else he was doing, take a train from Baltimore to Boston, and show up without an appointment and without the slightest certainty that anyone would even see him?

Greenfield had his answer ready. In fact, his answer was all but oozing from his pores. He grabbed the edge of the mahogany desk like a ship's rail and, white-knuckled, pulled himself forward. Why did he want in? *Why?!* Because he'd been thinking, and he'd been reading the papers, and, most important, he'd been *out there.* (Here he gestured through the Dean's window, as if the manicured grounds of Soldiers Field could fill in for the whole enormous postwar universe.) Yes, he'd been out in the world of ships and tinned food and supply lines, and he'd got a notion of what American know-how and American drive could do, and he didn't see any reason, now that peace had come, why America couldn't just keep doing more of the same and doing it better, better than anyone had ever done it anywhere; why industry couldn't crank up such a vast momentum that it would just steamroll over rough spots and fill in all the cracks like lava; why prosperity couldn't billow up into such a fat balloon that there was no corner of the country that it wouldn't fill, that there'd be no halfway deserving person who couldn't feed off that stupendous tenderloin. *That's* what the future could be like, if only people were heads-up about it, if only they didn't blow it, and he, Stanley Greenfield, wanted to be out there with the best training and the best credentials he could find, so that . . .

The Dean looked at his watch. "I have to go," he said.

"Which way are you going?" Stanley Greenfield asked.

On the Anderson Bridge, with elegant sculls slipping silently by on the river and prewar jalopies rolling noisily by on the road, Greenfield fleshed in his vision of steaming smokestacks and shiny new plants and homes going up by the millions. Up Boylston Street he sidestepped and shufflestepped, his taps scratching on the sidewalk, tracking the Dean like a terrier, rhapsodizing on the limitless promise of postwar America, vigorous, swelling, benign. And at Harvard Square, with the Dean about to slip away into the underground, maybe slip away forever, he put his palms up, craned his neck, and, in a tone that was almost that of prayer, said, "All I want is to be a part of that."

"Everyone wants to be a part of it," said the Dean. "We'll notify you."

two

The Making of
a Competent Elite

Herb Shayne arranged his shaving brush and mug on the shelf above the sink, dropped his toothbrush in the glass, and tried somehow to hide his allergy pills in the empty medicine cabinet. Then he walked back through his three-man suite in Hamilton Hall, flopped down on his bed, and bit the end off a cigar.

Shayne was twenty-two, Canadian, and had been too young for the war. He was uncomfortably tall and hopelessly thin, with bright red hair, a transparent skin that showed orange and bluish underneath, and a voice that skidded upward through the tenor range and cracked whenever he waxed emphatic. He didn't kid himself that smoking a cigar changed any of that. Still, a cigar seemed to help to keep him calm, and Herb Shayne was trying hard not to act ridiculous in front of the older guys about how tickled he was to find himself at Harvard.

He'd thought about it all his life. As a foreigner, he'd invested Harvard with the awe that Americans reserve for Oxford and the British feel for Heidelberg. Harvard, believed Herb Shayne, was where the exchange of thoughts had the profoundest resonance, where the intellectual rigor was most sublime. Harvard would be the perfect cask for the maturing of the raw ideas he'd picked up as an undergraduate at Montreal's McGill. Central among those ideas was the conviction that the discipline of economics, while its tools were numbers and equations, was in essence a thing of flesh and blood, of ethics and of soul; economics, in the actual practice of business no less than in theory, could be rightly understood only as a branch of moral philosophy. Herb Shayne could hardly wait to share this viewpoint with his B School roommates.

His roommates found it novel, mystifying, hilarious, and dimly subversive. *"Moral philosophy,* Herb?" they'd said. "Herb, we're not trying to get rid of you, but did it ever occur to you that maybe you're on the wrong side of the river?"

They had a point. Shayne had made it to Harvard, but he'd landed one trolley stop short of Cambridge, the place where the College of his fantasy, if it existed at all, was to be found. The Business School was on the Boston side, the city side, the side that was unabashedly of this world, and while it was built of the same crimson brick and understated Georgian facings, it was a rather different sort of place. The College cogitated through to logical conclusions; the Business School got results. That's why people went there.

It was certainly why the great majority of the 695 who entered in the fall of 1947 had come. They wanted good jobs. It was, for most, that simple. They'd grown up during the Great Depression. Eighty-six percent were veterans and had given an average of thirty-four months to the war. They shared a goading awareness of time lost, and, being in their twenties, they believed that lost time could somehow be recovered.

They were different, this group, from any that had come before. Harvard Business School had long claimed that no qualified applicant would be prevented from attending by financial limitations; now, with Uncle Sam footing the bills, that claim was coming considerably closer to being true. Not that the Class of '49 was exactly democratic. There was, at the demographic top of it, a group of neo-Fitzgeraldians who were the keepers of such B School traditions as the monogrammed bathrobe, the brushed-silver flask, and the nontaxability of the Clifford trust. More than one '49er in seven had a father who was chief of the company he worked for. Another 13 percent were the sons of men with businesses of their own. Only one '49er in twenty-five had a father who was a blue-collar worker. Of blacks or women there were none.

Still, 78 percent of the class attended with the help of GI benefits, and many of those would never have seen the inside of Harvard had the Japanese not attacked Pearl Harbor. They were sons of salesmen and farmers and bookkeepers. They came from inner-city public schools and second-tier Midwestern land-grant colleges, and they'd grown up in households where maiden aunts and union-member uncles still spoke Polish or Yiddish or Italian or Greek. They'd been outsiders before the war, but now, having put in their time and let themselves be shot at like everybody else, they were not to be denied a share in the rewards. They had no family firms to slide into, no preestablished networks of mentors to usher them along. What they did have, though, was the opportunity to try to make it on their own, and, in the name of that unprecedented chance, they brought to the Business School an almost hysterical intensity of effort that the blithe prewar preppies would have found eccentric, unbecoming, and terrifying.

In the fall of 1947 the reading load for first-year students was running about six hours a night. The students asked for more. Weekends were cut in half by reports that had to be handed in by precisely nine p.m. on Saturday. The students suggested that the papers might be more complete if they had Sunday to work on them as well. Finance, Production, Marketing, Control—they gobbled up the first-year curriculum as if it were made of beef.

But if the sheer volume of material was powerless to daunt them, the B School's policies regarding grades and feedback drove them to insomnia. The School seemed to operate on the premise that in the world of business you never quite knew where you stood, and you might as well get used to it. So, in class discussions, students would stick their necks out on flamboyant analyses, and the professors would give a neutral nod and call on someone else. Papers came back innocent of grades. At semester's end there'd be no satisfyingly specific As and Bs, but only the fuzzy Pass, High Pass, and Distinction. Nor would there be class rankings. The Class would simply be divided into thirds, with the top 5 percent—and nobody quite knew how they were picked—singled out as Baker Scholars.

The system struck the future MBAs as nothing short of diabolical. They'd been through enough uncertainty to last them a lifetime; now they were hankering for a sure thing, or at least a thing with hard edges, a game they could psych out and know they were winning. If they wanted haziness, they would have gone to a different school. So they protested. They argued with professors, they editorialized in the student paper, the *Harbus News*. Finally, just before Christmas of 1947, the Administration called a general meeting.

Associate Dean Stanley Teele went up to the podium and assured the student body that their complaints had been heard and their feelings carefully considered. Then he announced that nothing whatsoever was going to change.

Feet scraped on the floor. Fingers drummed on desks. Teele took off his rimless glasses, steamed them with his breath, and very deliberately mopped the lenses with an enormous linen handkerchief. He held the glasses up to the light till quiet grudgingly returned.

"But gents," he continued at last, "if you don't mind my saying so, I really think you're a bit more nervous than you need to be, and there are a couple of things I'd like to say that may help to put your minds at ease.

"All we do is divide the class up into thirds, that's true.

"But look, the Baker Scholars and the men in the top third of the class—they tend to go into research or to get good academic positions at which they distinguish themselves. So you don't have to worry if you're one of them.

"The men in the middle third, well, they tend to be the well-rounded types—good athletes, sociable, lots of friends—and they go on to do very nicely because they're such regular fellows. So you don't have to worry if you're one of them.

"And the men in the bottom third—well, they tend to get out of here and go make an awful lot of money. So the point, gentlemen, is this: you're at the Harvard Business School, and except for making damn sure you pass the course, you really don't have to lose any sleep about where you stand. Trust me."

Maybe they trusted him, maybe they didn't. Either way, his point about the secure glow that should come with a Harvard MBA could not have been better taken. In 1949, dramatically more so than today, that degree packed a wallop.

As of that year, there were only fifty thousand living MBAs of any vintage, from any school, in the entire nation.* Not only was the MBA degree rare, it was arcane. Professional management, at the time, was a subject which, to the average joe, was only slightly less abstruse than quantum physics, but which seemed a good deal more important. An MBA guaranteed penetration into a body of almost sacred knowledge, and it did so at a historical moment when the prestige, as well as the commodity value, of management skill had never been higher. Faith arrives in a flash; skepticism takes time; and in 1949 faith in modern rational management—*American* management—was new, axiomatic, and utterly untarnished.

American management, after all, had just won the war. Sure, the movies always zeroed in on three handsome

---

* In 1985 alone, more than sixty thousand new MBAs were awarded.

GIs capturing an island or tunneling out of a prison camp with a spoon, but that was pap for the masses. Patriotism aside, you couldn't really say the Americans were better soldiers than the Germans; you couldn't keep a straight face while asserting that they were braver or more determined than the Japanese. No, anybody who understood the war effort realized that it had been a matter of goods and services. The Americans had come out on top because their materiel got produced in staggering volume and almost always ended up where it was needed. The U.S. war machine had been the world's goingest operation—and what worked amidst the bowel-loosening pressures of combat would surely work in the luxurious calm of peace. American management savvy would guarantee economic supremacy just as it had masterminded military dominion.

The only real question was whether there was enough management savvy to go around. Given the postwar era's ever increasing emphasis on specialization, the mystery, in fact, was how America had blundered through to world hegemony in the first place, with such a conspicuous shortage of experts. In any event, the year 1949, for people with a degree that indicated they knew how to make things go, offered a seller's market the likes of which will not be seen again.

The season's entire nationwide MBA harvest was 3,900—and one out of six of them was a Harvard man. It is only very recently that HBS grads have come to be perceived as a small, select group at the top of a broad and lofty pyramid; in 1949, and for some time afterward, the Harvard men stood out by their sheer numbers. That year there were fewer than 100 institutions dispensing MBAs, as opposed to nearly 700 in 1985, and not one of them produced a bigger graduating class than Harvard. Further, when it came time to invoke the old school ties, the Harvard men had an incalculable edge—nearly *half* of the MBAs already ensconced in business were of Harvard stock, because Harvard had virtually invented the MBA degree.* Far from being a boutique, the B school was the Ohio State of commerce, turning out winning teams—in part, at least, because it had the biggest student body from which it could recruit.

It also, in 1947, seemed to have the most spirited student body, owing to the criteria by which that year's entering class had been selected.

The admissions people had a problem on their hands that year. It was considered bad form to talk about it, since there'd been a war on, after all, and it really wasn't anybody's fault. Still, there was no getting around the fact that, in purely academic terms, the guys who'd earned their bachelor's degrees on either end of the conflict were possibly the most spottily educated bunch ever to be handed sheepskins. In '41 and '42 able-bodied sophomores had spent more time on drill parade than in the library, then been given two years' worth of college credits and bundled off to fight. If they made it back, they were squeezed through wildly accelerated third- and fourth-year programs whose true purpose was to clear the lecture halls for the unprecedented tens of thousands coming up behind, compliments of the GI Bill. The meaning of de-

---

* HBS, in fact, was the *second* school devoted to business education at the graduate level. Dartmouth's Amos Tuck school, which opened its doors in 1900, anticipated Harvard by eight years. Harvard has not gone out of its way to publicize this fact; less understandably, neither, apparently, has Tuck.

grees grew hazy. A BS in engineering might have meant you'd studied weapons trajectories; working on the supply lines probably geared you up for marketing. As for such contemplative and unpragmatic subjects as literature or philosophy, who'd had time for them?

At the Business School the problem was exacerbated by the fact that from 1942 to 1946 the MBA program had been suspended altogether while the faculty worked with the military on managing the war effort. By 1947, then, the B School had not one year's worth of applicants, but *five* years' worth, and it lacked a clear-cut policy about how to choose among them. Undergraduate transcripts were a farce. Standardized entrance exams didn't yet exist. Everybody could pay, and only so many slots could decently be reserved for sons of old alums or of actual or prospective benefactors.

So the admissions people had no choice but to go by the one thing they could concretely size up and appraise: the candidate himself, generally as he came across in a thirty-minute interview—his presentation, his salesmanship, his spiel. What they were looking for was confidence, certainty, the kind of quick, aggressive poise that the B School couldn't teach. The trick was to convey gumption in an instant and never shrink from gumption's hale high pitch. Qualities of mind and traits of character that couldn't be made so immediately apparent just couldn't be factored in. It wasn't the admissions people's fault. There was a lot of improvising to be done in the conversion back to peacetime, and it was improvising under pressure, with everybody in a hurry. So the B School couldn't guarantee that it would end up with a high percentage of scholars, much less visionaries; the most it could promise was that it would filter out the wimps. The sciences could have the starry-eyed introverts. Arts and letters could take the subtle brooders who reveled in the shades of gray. Modern American business was to be carried on the shoulders of a different type, the type who knew exactly what he wanted and would march on straight ahead to get it. So the Business School would claim the action guys. The Business School would get results.

Herb Shayne, in that interminable, vacant summer before Harvard, had read the B School catalog cover to cover and back again. He took it to the park with him until his hay fever got unbearable. Then he read it in his room, with the electric fan turning side to side in front of the window, and his bare feet dangling over the end of his bed. Parts of the catalog he memorized. He wanted to be ready for the jargon they'd throw at him down at Soldiers Field. More than that, he just loved the serious sound of the course descriptions.

Human Relations, for example, promised to promote on-the-job goodwill by addressing "the problems of securing cooperative action . . . [regarding] the specialized functions of personnel." The Advertising seminar would probe to the heart of common needs by focusing "especial attention . . . [on] the habits and behavior of consumers whom advertising is designed to influence." Then there was an elective whose very name—Public Relations and Responsibilities—bespoke a social awareness and commitment that was the very stuff of an enlightened approach to business.

But those, of course, were the orthodox, approved descriptions, and, as Herb Shayne learned when he was actually installed at HBS, one thing could be described in many different ways. Around the dorm, for example, the gist of Human Relations was summarized as "making the contented-cow syndrome work for you." The meat of Advertising lay in "teaching the native to want." And in the classroom, as Shayne would remember decades later, "PR & R, when it dealt with anything at all, usually addressed questions like whether you'd generate more business by heading up the United Way or being president of the local Rotary."

What all of this suggested is that two different educations were being offered at the Business School. One was official, the other was real, and the two were held together, sort of, by the pedagogical technique known as case method—a teaching strategy that has become synonymous with the Business School itself.

Case method was supposed to bridge the gap between business theory, which was respectable, and business practice, which made money. By "solving" anecdotal problems drawn from the histories of real-world companies, students could get comfy with the decision-making habits of top management while at the same time remaining cognizant of the theoretical concerns that top management too often didn't have time for. The idea was fine, except for the fact that business theory was pallid, pompous, and usually self-evident, while business practice was gripping, human-scaled, endlessly compelling in its stakes-on-the-table actuality. So theory got short shrift. In Manufacturing, for example, once you'd got the concepts of long runs and economies of scale, what else was there to say about theory? On the other hand, one could easily spend a semester listening to charismatic professor General Georges Doriot spin French-accented yarns about cases in which "a single zhenious of an industrial spy could pruhve more valuable zan an entire research laboratry."

But if case method didn't necessarily keep the abstract and the concrete in balance, it at least fostered a point of view. The view was bird's-eye, since in real life no one except a company's top two or three executives would be faced with decisions of the kind that B School students were routinely asked to deal with. "It was great daydream material," Herb Shayne remembers. "The case would open, 'You are the chairman of the XYZ Corporation,' and, *poof,* just like that you're chairman of the board. We had lots of cases about dealing with subordinates. I don't think we had one about dealing with a boss. The assumption, from the first day on, was that we'd *be* the boss. The analogy would be studying freshman Poli Sci from the perspective of a future king."

The approach was not to everybody's taste. It was not, daydreams aside, particularly to Herb Shayne's, and one day in the spring of 1948, his enthusiasm tempered, his liberal instincts affronted, he found himself sitting at the edge of the B School quad, gazing absently toward Cambridge. He lit up a cigar and watched the boats go by on the Charles. He mocked himself with snippets of the catalog blather he still could quote verbatim. He must have looked unhappy, because a classmate of his named Conrad Jones came over and asked him what was wrong. Shayne tried to put his finger on it, and came around to a voice-cracking complaint against what he saw as the Busy School's elitism.

Now, Connie Jones, who was square-built and had

been away to war and had an engineering degree from
Purdue, would end up being the senior partner of the New
York consulting firm of Booz, Allen and Hamilton. Consulting would fit him like a glove because he had a gift for
telling people things they didn't want to hear and ending
up having them thank him for it. It wasn't that Connie
Jones was gentle in delivery, or even tactful exactly, but
that there was about him a profound neutrality that
seemed the very soul of justice. Devoid of malice, sparing
in affection, he called them as he saw them, and he proceeded to tell Herb Shayne that he was full of shit.

"No, Herb," he said, "it doesn't bother you at all that
we're treated as an elite. What bothers you is that we're
not the elite you thought we were going to be. You thought
we were going to be the intellectual elite. Well, we're not.
We're not the hereditary elite, and we're certainly not the
artistic or creative elite. What we're being groomed as is
the competent elite. Get used to it, Herb—we're being
trained to be the guys who stay sober at the party. We're
being handed the tools to get out there and run things."

That, finally, was the crux of the B School exercise, and of
all the tools the Class of '49 was handed, the most versatile
by far was contained in the course called Administrative
Practices. Ad Prac was the glue that held the rest of the
curriculum together, the section of the kit that held the
master plan. Other courses taught you a lot of what and at
least a little bit of why. The beauty part of Ad Prac was that
it had a way of making those preoccupations disappear, so
that pure, unadulterated how came shining through. Ad
Prac, like aspirin or like dynamite, would work on just
about anything.

The catalog described the course's aim as teaching the future manager "to obtain action by working through people . . . [by] maintaining harmony between the individuals and groups of which his organization is composed . . . [and by] utiliz [ing] the capacities of the individuals concerned to the greatest advantage." The students were terser. They dubbed the class Machiavelli for Beginners. It was leadership and gamesmanship, politics, negotiation, hardball, and the end run. Future conglomerateur Harry Figgie, Jr., summed up its lesson as "how to saw the rungs out of someone's ladder without his even knowing it."

So central was Ad Prac to the B School way of doing things that the phrase soon overwhelmed its boundaries as a noun and began being used in various forms as a transitive verb, a past participle, and an adjective. You could ad-prac the mailman into stamping a fraudulent postmark on a tardily finished report. A fellow who'd been finagled into doing more than his fair share of work on a group project had been ad-prac'd. Wellesley girls were now and then ad-pracable, and even B School professors could occasionally be cast as ad-prac-ees. Ad Prac was more than a method, it was a world view, the unbleeding heart of the B School ethos. It was the armor you put on when, come hell, high water, or the Democrats, something just had to get done.

Ad Prac, in fact, was almost a religion. The Harvard MBAs of 1949 seemed early on to have an inkling that their destiny would be something special, something worth keeping tabs on, and even before they'd set forth from Soldiers Field they'd started doing surveys on themselves. In the year of their graduation they took a poll as to their collective ideologies. Three quarters of the men of '49 testified to a belief in God. Ninety-two point five percent proclaimed a faith in the effective wisdom of Administrative Practices. Ad Prac was Gospel, it was Torah, it was Tao. It was the austere, pragmatic, and unrelenting creed by which they were setting out to manage America.

three

Out of the Frying Pan . . .

Ned Dewey found himself with plenty of time to read the paper, but the paper mostly aggravated him. True, the U.S., for the moment, was firmly ensconced on top of the world. In 1949 one half of all the goods made, grown, or mined on planet Earth were American. The average Yank had an income that was fifteen times greater than the average foreigner's, and he ate three and a half times as much as was normal for the human race. Henry Luce had gazed out from his pulpit atop Time-Life and dubbed the era that was dawning "the American Century." It was a ringing phrase if ever there was one, but Ned Dewey didn't buy the idea that absolutely everything was peachy. China all of a sudden was Communist. The Russians all of a sudden had the atom bomb. Truman, in a spasm of generosity, was throwing money all over Europe, lavishing

Band-Aids on Japan, and had just decided, in a policy that the papers called Point Four, that it would be a swell idea to share American technology, free of charge, with the whole wide struggling world. As a thank you, the Greeks had just renamed the main commercial boulevard in Athens, Uncle Harry Street. That was world politics in a nutshell, thought Ned Dewey: we give them a zillion dollars in aid, they spend eleven drachmas changing street signs to honor a guy who should never have been President in the first place.

So to hell with the news. To pass the time, sitting there in oily khakis in the Gulf station on the southern fringe of Harlem, Dewey took greater amusement from thinking about how his job description would read, had his job been graced by a description: *Employee shall burn hands on oil dipsticks and scrape bird-do off of windshields, with squeegee if possible, with fingernail if necessary; employee shall grease axles and forearms, and maintain sanitary conditions in restrooms, nausea notwithstanding; employee shall maintain fatuous smile while distributing road maps and may assist in minor repairs if deemed competent to do so by sadistic chief mechanic. Wages: a buck an hour, before taxes, zilch extra for evenings or weekends. Advanced degree from major Eastern university required.* Yes, sir, Ned Dewey told himself, it was quite a job he'd landed; this oil game was pretty terrific, and he didn't mind having pulled a few strings to get in on it.

But no, he admitted, that was an exaggeration, that was swagger. He hadn't really pulled strings. It was more a matter of just being in a certain place at a certain time, having people know your name and having it linked in their minds with certain other names. Like, someone might meet him and say, "Ned Dewey, Ned Dewey—weren't you part of that old Harvard football team with that Kennedy boy on it?" Well, Dewey could hardly deny it. Yeah, he and Bobby had tickled the pigskin together, were quite good friends in fact. RFK, undersized, quietly ferocious, and about as loose-hipped as the white boys in the Ivy League ever got, had played split end; Ned Dewey, square-built, gruff, with ready elbows and a battered nose, had held down the middle of the line. He'd given his knees for Alma Mater, in fact, but on balance it was worth it; wrecked knees were one of those jock intangibles that you got a lot of mileage out of in later life. It was probably football, Ned Dewey acknowledged, that had got him into Business School. Besides, old grads loved to talk to football players, buttonholed them every chance they got. The conversation was always the same: two questions about the gridiron exploits of the younger man, followed by an endless play-by-play of the 1921 Dartmouth game, followed, now and then at least, by a veiled or naked offer of a job.

It didn't hurt, either, that Dewey's father had been a distinguished economist, a pioneer, even though he'd ended up with one of history's more embarrassing jobs: Dewey Senior had been the Hoover administration's leading authority on what was then the shiny new subject of business cycles. Dewey Senior shrugged a lot. That's how his son remembered him—shrugging, squaring papers on a desktop, and puzzling over the seeming disappearance of half the money in the world.

Still, a high-level government background, a crimson letter in football, and a Harvard MBA—it was a potent combination for a son just setting out to cut his own swath through the world. Put all those advantages together and you got . . . what? A job as a trainee with Gulf Oil, pumping gas into Negroes' cars on the wrong end of Central Park. Well, in 1949 even Harvard MBAs tended to start out in the field, at the point where the product met the customer and revenues came in fifty cents at a time. Besides, Dewey couldn't deny that he was learning things they hadn't taught him up at Soldiers Field: he could now construct oil-can pyramids with the best of them; he could change a pair of wiper blades in fifteen seconds flat.

Then there was this fellow named Ernie Mitchell, a Baker Scholar who found himself working at a Midwestern factory that made bread wrappers. Mitchell's father, too, had been in government service, though in a somewhat different capacity. He'd set out to be a career naval officer, but decided, after twenty years, that he'd had enough of that. The decision was poorly timed. It was 1930, and the elder Mitchell, by default, eventually found himself back on the federal payroll. This time he was part of a WPA crew that carried enormous rocks and implanted them in the banks of the Mississippi, the idea being to prevent the North American continent and its vastest river from getting in each other's way. It dawned on little Ernie at an early age that he should do his very best at school.

Fastidious, quiet, with a pug face and a prematurely chastened gaze, Ernie Mitchell was every teacher's favorite poor but striving kid, the type they were always trying to help without humiliating, somehow getting him a new suit for the science fair, a fresh pair of shoes for the finals of the spelling bee. He ended up winning a scholarship to Harvard College. The GI Bill sent him to the Business

School, where he was one of the very hottest guys. In his second year he did a project on atomic energy, and he interviewed Oppenheimer and Teller, he spoke to Einstein on the phone; Einstein, his mind, perhaps, on other things, kept thinking Mitchell was his Christian name. The only source who couldn't make time to talk to him was the President of the United States.

Upon graduation Ernie Mitchell could have gone to work for almost any business in America. He went to the Waxide Paper Company, in Kansas City, as an assistant plant manager. He worked on the shop floor amid the clang of machinery and the stink of wax being bonded onto paper and of ink being processed onto wax. "Look," he says, "I could've had more glamorous jobs, I could've gone somewhere where they dealt in bigger numbers and where I could've had an office with a window. But what I liked about Waxide was that it was basic. We made a product that let people eat fresher bread, period.

"And I'll tell you another thing," says Ernie Mitchell. "I tell this to younger people in business, and they look at me like I'm either kidding them or getting senile: I took that job because it was the savviest move I could've made at the time. People don't seem to see it this way anymore, but industry *happens* on the shop floor. In 1949, operations was where the action was, it's what business was *about,* and it was the surest route to the top of a company. That was the logic we were taught, and that was the logic that worked."

By that logic Mitchell went on to become president and CEO of Crown Zellerbach International, a $3.1 billion operation.

*   *   *

But the game, from top to bottom, was somewhat different then.

An executive job in 1949 wasn't necessarily thought of as a job done sitting down, and an MBA degree didn't necessarily suggest a lifetime of clean fingernails. American enterprise was seen as the apotheosis of the Yankee tinkerer, and wealth was created not by fancy math and the cutting of deals, but by the conceiving, making, and selling of products for a marketplace. And in the name of keeping the widgets scudding past on the conveyor belts, it seemed natural to the postwar men of business that they might have to start their careers in some uncosmopolitan place, suck a little shop-floor dust into their lungs, and deal firsthand with the bitching of customers or of shop stewards. That went for entry-level managers straight out of the service; it went for Harvard MBAs. Elite or otherwise, they couldn't afford to play the prima donna, the egghead, or the fop. National consensus as to what was fit and proper for a man to do made those poses utterly untenable.

The American philosophy of the day was blunt and literal; the common faith and the common yearning were for things you could hold in your hand. The present called for hard work so that the near future would contain overflowing bags of groceries and kitchen counters full of small appliances. It was a vision conditioned by the Depression and by wartime shortages, and it would be realized now by stouthearted adherence to a sort of Postwar Code, a set of values that was never quite spelled out and didn't need to be, so thorough and osmotic was its influence. The Code fitted perfectly the contours of the postwar moment, and that was the best and worst thing about it. The Code was bighearted and arrogant, optimistic, noble, and naïve. It celebrated American preeminence, and the feats of body, mind, and spirit that had made that ascendance happen; but already it took American preeminence for granted, as if it were the culmination of history, rather than an episode in the ongoing dynamic among nations.

The Code has as its major premise that the Americans were the effective guys, the good guys, and it set the framework for what being a good guy, in business and in life, was all about. The good guys never let their buddies down, they married the girl if they got her in trouble, and they thought nothing of getting elbow-deep in grease if something needed fixing. The good guys played by the rules, but might stretch them now and then because rules were based on how things had been done before, not on how they had to be done forever. The good guys were allowed a certain amount of bragging and of bluster, but they never said anything they weren't ready to back up with sweat, with loyalty, and with cash on the line. The good guys believed that ambition itself was somehow patriotic. They didn't ask for outside help and they stayed on the job till the job was done.

That was the staunch and hands-on ethos that was shaping American life and American enterprise at mid-century, and the Harvard MBAs of '49 would be among its most steadfast keepers. They believed, for example, that a businessman wasn't quite compleat if he couldn't take apart and put together the widget he made his living off of, and they themselves were a group at ease with a screwdriver. More than a third of the Class—by far the largest single group—had majored in engineering as undergraduates. At the Business School, 24 percent made Production their area of concentration. The next-largest group chose

Marketing, on the belief that if you weren't going to make something, then you ought at least to sell something. Only 13.7 percent chose Finance, which has more recently become the B School's most heavily subscribed course.* By the wisdom of the Postwar Code, however, diddling with numbers was for accountants, for fidgeters, for guys who lacked that vague but crucial quality known as grit. *Real* businessmen worked with people and with merchandise; real businessmen were out there in the streaming, face-to-face world where business actually happened.

Nor was finance the only latterly fashionable field that the men of '49 thought of as unworthy.

Take consulting. In 1985 more than a dozen management consulting firms recruited at the Harvard Business School, and nearly a quarter of the graduating class signed up with them. In 1949 *zero* consulting operations went fishing at the School, and *zero* grads became consultants (though around twenty have since moved on to that profession, the majority as a halfway measure toward retirement). In 1949 consulting was an infant industry, devoid of glamour and shaky on its legs; it also seemed to be essentially a scam. Who needed consultants? And why? If management was doing its job, you didn't have to bring in extra suits to look over its shoulder. And if management *wasn't* doing its job, didn't it make more sense to purge the team than to hire outside brooms to keep the fungus under the rug? At best, management consultants duplicated effort; at worst, they conspired in screwing up;

---

* By 1985, "areas of concentration" had been defined out of the B School curriculum. The School's four most popular courses, however, were Analysis of Corporate Financial Reports, Capital Markets, Corporate Financial Management, and Entrepreneurial Finance.

either way, by the criteria of 1949, minding someone else's business was a distant second choice to having your own to mind.

For not dissimilar reasons, the Class of '49 showed a marked aversion to Wall Street. In 1985 nearly 28 percent of HBS's new grads flocked to the Street, which had by then become the highest-paying and most prestigious venue for young go-getters. Among the Class of '49 less than 1 percent—six guys!—went to work there. The other 99 percent held their noses when they passed it on the subway. In 1949 Wall Street was from hunger, a backwater of the action and a haven for well-connected mediocrities. You proved yourself unfit for more manly occupations and Popsy would buy you a seat on the Exchange. It would keep you out of trouble, and you could make yourself somewhat useful as the errand boy, at least, of those who were actually *doing* something. Not that you'd ever make much money. Trading volume on the Big Board was averaging a whopping 600,000 shares a day.

Investment banking was not particularly more exciting than shuffling shares. The field was little publicized in 1949 and tended to be talked about in slightly guilty whispers, as if large amounts of borrowed money connoted something *ipso facto* shady. Besides, depending on who you asked, the industry was tainted either by too much Jewishness or by endemic anti-Semitism. As for venture capital, that seemed *really* sleazy; the very phrase conjured up images of oily men with pinkie rings carrying briefcases full of unmarked cash. No, in 1949, if you were serious about finding a niche in mainstream, respectable, *productive* business, you didn't want to go to Wall Street. The game was rather different then.

Not that the typical '49er was a guy who went to seek his fortune among the smokestacks of the hinterlands. No, the largest single group of grads—around 40 percent—did end up in New York, for the same simple reason that Willie Sutton robbed banks: it was where the money was. For the Class of 1949, though, New York didn't mean downtown and finance; it meant midtown and marketing. Marketing was the next logical step in the increasing abstraction of business, and in 1949 the marketing guys could think of themselves as fleet and nimble halfbacks who would take the ball from the signal-callers of production and carry it down the field.

The word on everybody's lips was growth, and it was growth that dictated the strategy by which business deployed its talents. With the economic pie swelling apace, what you wanted to do was claim a share of a market with a solid product, then widen your slice with savvy selling. It was a waste to put the good minds on the financial side— business hadn't yet become *that* abstract—because the ledger would take care of itself as the pie expanded.

Savvy selling, however, was easier said than done, because in 1949, rather suddenly, there were more goods on the market than there had ever been before. Factories were still cranked up to wartime levels of production, and in the general frenzy to alleviate recent shortages and cash in while prices were still high, just about everybody had overshot the mark. Inventories grew mountainous and cash flow stank. Accordingly, there dawned the golden age of the one-cent sale, the kamikaze price war, the wacko promotion that threw in a side of Texas beef for anyone who'd buy a freezer. Competition was murderous, but it was all *domestic* competition, and, as in penny poker among the family, everybody knew the money would end up back in the selfsame cupboard at the end of the game. So why not raise, bluff, and generally play it to the hilt? In 1949 Columbia Records cut the legs off the market for 78s by introducing the first LPs; RCA ad-prac'd them by inventing the 45, playable, as it happened, only on Radio Corp's own Victrola. General Cigar wreaked havoc on the easy arithmetic of the dime panatela by offering one that cost nine cents. GE, Philco, and Admiral, meanwhile, were fighting over the nascent market for television sets with such abandon that in one year prices fell by more than a third. Asked to describe the relationship between Admiral and its competitors, that company's chief responded with a smile: "We hate them and they hate us."

It was a mud bath, and no mistake. It was also a time when modern, quantitative marketing techniques were still struggling after credibility, and that's where the Harvard MBAs came in. The new grads had the up-to-the-minute jargon, the reassuring confidence, and the impeccable wing-tip shoes, and marketing needed them badly. The infant industry of Market Research needed them, because Market Research—unaided by computers and still groping toward consensus on the most basic issues of sampling and validity—was still trying to convince a skeptical world that it had anything to sell. The gray giants of Packaged Goods needed them, because in fields where virtually identical products went head-to-head, the smarts of the brand manager could make the crucial difference; as many '49s went to Lever Brothers alone as to all of Wall Street.

Most of all, though, it was the ad agencies of 1949 that needed the Harvard MBAs, because Madison Avenue was trying desperately to shed the slime of its medicine-show huckster past and reposition itself as respectable. The ad biz had never been deficient in creativity; if anything, it had suffered from an excess of imagination, which some people were unkind enough to interpret as tendencies toward willful fraud. Now the agencies were after some cool, poised Ivy League types to balance out the wild-eyed concept men and the frazzled-genius art directors. In 1949, for the first time ever, Madison Avenue went to Soldiers Field to recruit, and walked away with a couple of dozen of the season's brightest prospects.

"Account exec," intones Herb Shayne, one of six guys signed up by the firm of McCann, Erickson, Incorporated; "it's a tired, tarnished title now maybe, but in 1949 it was a phrase to conjure with, a job that put you squarely in the middle of the action. From then right through the fifties, being an account exec seemed as racy and modern as a skinny tie."

If it's true that the most exciting business to be in at a given time is the business that's changing the most, then in 1949 Madison Avenue was in fact the place to be. As of 1948, Advertising was a mere $650 million industry, and virtually an invisible one; it played the traditional wife to Manufacturing's traditional husband; its role was to support and never to upstage. By 1960, ad revenues had ballooned to nearly $12 billion and advertising itself had become one of the dominant features on the American scene. Boschian renderings of Tension, Pressure, and Pain; airborne fantasies of Hertz putting *you* in the driver's seat—the hooks for the products gradually became more compelling than the products. Advertising gradually supplanted Production as the hot spot in the process of moving goods—the halfbacks, that is, were usurping the quarterbacks. In the short run at least, the strategy worked fine. A product, after all, was invented only once, but selling was forever.

"What's hard to get across," Herb Shayne continues, "is the sheer manic invigoration of those days, how happy you were to be putting in a sixty-hour week for sixty dollars take-home pay. You'd get up at seven, shock yourself awake with a big splash of after-shave, and head for the crush of the subway. By eight-thirty you'd be looking at story boards and feeling like one hell of a versatile character—swapping concepts with the creatives, talking budgets with the client, playing go-between for the media buyers and sellers who haggled like Turks over a rug. Lunch would be gin and gossip—a never-ending *torrent* of gossip: every day some account getting yanked, some vice-president jumping ship. And then those closed-door meetings at the agency, figuring out how to goose the client to spend a little more, and then a little more again."

Shayne's voice still skids upward as he speaks, but it doesn't crack anymore; he's got the knack of wryly breaking off just at the topmost limit of his range. He's still got red hair, though it's bleaching out toward silver now, and he's nearly as lean as he was at Business School. In the early sixties he became what he calls "an executive son-in-law," and now presides over a $50 million diversified family company called Werthan Industries down in Tennessee.

"So you'd stay at the office till six-thirty or seven," he remembers, "and then it would be time to relax, right? Wrong. You'd walk through Times Square and the fruits of your labors would hit you in the face. There'd be billboards blowing gigantic smoke rings, Coke bottles eight stories high pouring soda into enormous neon glasses, 3-D boxes of Oxydol hanging from the roofs. You couldn't get away from it, and you didn't *want* to."

Why get away from it? It was, after all, what the men of '49 had been waiting for, hoping for, grooming themselves to grab a piece of. If anything could compensate them for the time they'd lost, it could only be this general picking up of the pace, this cheerfully surreal explosion of the scale of things.

"What made it all the sweeter," says Herb Shayne, tenderly rolling the tip of his cigar against the marble ashtray, "is that in our heart of hearts we didn't really think things would turn out as well as they did. We talked big, but there was a lot of pure bravado in that. Look at what we were used to—first lousy times, then scary times, plus the awareness, if not the memory, of how the *last* postwar boom had ended up. So, bravado aside, our expectations were pretty modest. For better or worse, we did a lot to raise expectations for the batches that came after. But for us? We wanted a job that wouldn't bore us to death and that paid enough money and had enough security so that we could afford to have a family. That was really the meat of it. Anything past that came as a surprise. Anything past that was gravy."

four

... And into the Gravy

The median starting salary for the Harvard Business School Class of '49 was $3,600 a year. That's $300 a month or roughly $70 a week, and even adjusted for inflation, the annual figure comes to not much over $15,000.* Still, as Ernie Henderson, the Class Secretary and the son of the founder of Sheraton Hotels, affirms, "Every one of us was overpaid, relative to the guys to the right and left of us."

They were overpaid because their graduate degree, to the average employer, was worth maybe ten bucks extra a week, or twenty cents more per hour, based on the fifty-hour schedule that was roughly the Class norm. No big deal; but those two thin dimes were sufficient to set in mo-

---

* The median starting salary for 1985's Business School graduates was roughly $45,000.

tion a snowballing illogic whose cumulative effects would eventually be counted in the tens if not the hundreds of millions of dollars.

"If you grant the first premise," says Henderson, "then the rest more or less makes sense. Since we were overpaid, we had to be given more responsibility to justify it. Since we'd been given more responsibility, we had to be more closely watched by our bosses—and the best shortcut to that first promotion is making sure the boss man knows who the hell you are. The best shortcut to the *second* promotion, of course, is the first promotion. So you get the picture. Three, four years down the road, somebody back in the home office, who doesn't know jack-all about you or your work, looks up from his coffee and says, 'Jesus Christ, this guy isn't even out of his twenties and he's six levels up. He must be a real mover.' So you're a fast horse because they've *made* you a fast horse, and right away you're off to the races."

It helped, of course, to have a fast track to race on. As the fifties were getting under way, American economic growth was humping along at a hefty and reliable 4 percent a year. For nearly a quarter of a century, with only minor breathing spaces here and there, that level of expansion was going to hold rock-solid. The civilian labor force, meanwhile, was burgeoning. Between 1950 and 1955 more than three million new employees claimed a paycheck, creating a situation that stood the classic organizational pyramid on its head: weirdly but undeniably, there suddenly seemed to be more room at the top of the system than at the bottom.

A whole new socioeconomic category was surging into being in those halcyon days. The group thought of themselves as Junior Executives; William H. Whyte dubbed them Organization Men. They had flat-top haircuts, they shaved with electric razors that worked off the cigarette lighters of their Ramblers or De Sotos, and they carried attaché cases made of stuff that looked like leather. Depending on your point of view, they were either the sane and solid building-blocks of a new suburban utopia—"a Russia, only with money," as the saying went—or insidiously neutral clones who would be happily fiddling in their Black & Decker basement workshops as *1984* arrived. Either way, they flooded the entry levels of American business in such unprecedented numbers that they exerted a tremendous *upward* pressure on anyone above them in the hierarchy—even those who were only a year or two their senior, or who had started, for example, at two dimes more per hour.

Because of a unique set of historical flukes, there was a lack of corresponding downward pressure that would have kept the postwar movers sandwiched in the middle. To a remarkable degree, the men who occupied the plusher chairs in American business in the early 1950s were the same men who'd sat there as long ago as 1929. During the Depression, executives had lashed themselves to their desks like Ulysses to his mast, and just hoped they'd be able to ride out the storm. Little new blood came in through the thirties, and, with business prospects so dim, it was mainly dim prospects who studied business; the field's prestige had never been so low. During the war the training of civilian managers, and not only at Harvard, had essentially come to a standstill. The '49ers, then, emerged after a virtual twenty-year hiatus in the nurturing of managerial talent. There was a ground swell underneath them and a vacuum above, and, as HBS economic historian Alfred Chandler would put the matter: "There was not a comparable class, in terms of coming in on the brink of such opportunity and prosperity, in all of American history."

But if mere circumstance played a considerable role in the '49ers' general rise, circumstance alone cannot explain the particular orbits traced out by some of the class's highest flyers. As of 1954, for example, Tom Sawyer Murphy was earning around seven grand as a product manager for Lever Brothers. In 1983 he was America's fourth-highest-paid executive, pulling down, in salary and bonuses, $6,083,000 as chairman of Capital Cities Communications. In 1985 he became the first person ever to buy a television network, as Cap Cities performed the unlikely feat of acquiring ABC, an outfit four times its size.

It was on Labor Day of '54 that things got cooking for Murphy. He was at a party on Quaker Hill in Pawling, New York, a community of columned houses, wraparound verandas, and driveways measured in furlongs. His father, a State Supreme Court judge, played golf and talked politics up there with neighbors like Thomas E. Dewey, Edward R. Murrow, Norman Vincent Peale, and the financier–adventurer Lowell Thomas. It was one of those bright September days when lawns are moist and shadows cool as cotton quilts, and on Quaker Hill, dressed in lightweight flannels and bunting-striped straw boaters, the gathered friends proposed a toast to the American worker, albeit *in absentia.* Young Murphy, too, raised a glass. He dressed a bit more voguishly than others at the party, was already beginning to sport the pastel shirts and narrower lapels just then coming into style. Still, he was one of the group's more solid sons, realistic in his thinking, civil company for eighteen holes, not the dreamy, vague bohemian type who'd be off on some *amour* when he could be availing himself of the wisdom and experience of certain interesting gentlemen.

One such gentleman was an entrepreneur named Frank Smith, a man who on that Labor Day "was thinking of starting a little business with some friends" and was looking for a bright, ambitious fellow to help him run it. Did young Tom know of such a man, Frank Smith was asking? Maybe someone with a degree from one of the better business schools and some experience in marketing? Someone with the social graces who could talk to people, who would get on—someone rather like Tom Murphy himself?

The venture in question was the takeover of a small TV-and-radio station in Albany, and most of the investors were right there on that porch on Quaker Hill. Not that Frank Smith wanted to exaggerate the grandeur of the enterprise. The market served by the station—Albany-Troy-Schenectady—was unofficially referred to as the Tri-Slum region. The broadcast studio, such as it was, was housed in a converted nuns' residence. The last group who'd had the business had gone belly-up after losing money in a manner suggestive of arterial bleeding. Still, Frank Smith believed, the broadcast business was one that seemed to have some interesting times ahead of it.

"It's a crapshoot, is what it is," confessed the older man. "But it's a great opportunity for a young fellow. If we do well, you can make maybe a quarter-million in five years. If we go broke, you've got a great experience under your belt and plenty of time to apply it elsewhere. Think

about it." And Frank Smith wafted off in the wake of a silver tray of gin and tonics. He wasn't the type to bully
someone into an overhasty answer.

So Murphy thought. He was pretty happy where he
was. He had a good job with a crackerjack company in
what was then the flashiest building on Park Avenue. He
had his buddies in Manhattan, and for a young single guy
with some folding money to spend—well, the city had its
advantages. Whereas, Albany? He tried to picture Albany,
and what he saw was tire chains clanking over dirty snow,
lonely beers in badly lit bowling alleys amid the cheesy
smell of rented shoes. On the other hand, a dinky TV station on the skids, coming at you from a shack where nuns
used to live—this had a certain romance to it, this jibed
very nicely with the postwar notion of getting your hands
on something that was practically nothing and doing
something great with it. Murphy could picture himself
working in the shadow of a rickety transmission tower,
finding his way in the predawn hours by the flashing red
light meant to fend off low-flying planes. It conjured
images of Lindbergh, leather jackets with upturned collars, heroism in far-flung outposts. And let's face it, Frank
Smith didn't make bad investments very often. Guys who
did tended not to end up munching finger sandwiches on
Quaker Hill. Murphy took the job.

He moved upstate, where his first executive duty was
to paint the erstwhile convent. Then he sat in the snow
and wondered why he'd come. In its first year of operation
the new business lost $360,000, or roughly 15 percent of
the investment that had launched it. The problem, basically, was that advertisers didn't see the sense of spending
money on messages that vanished into thin air the instant

they'd been spoken; where did your jingle *go,* after all, once the tune had ended and the bouncing ball had bounced off the edge of the screen? So Murphy pined for Clarke's at happy hour and tried to remember where he'd put his résumé. Frank Smith was undaunted; in fact, like certain boxers who seem positively cheered up by taking a good one on the chin, he was encouraged. In 1956 he convinced his investors to cough up some more cash, and acquired two additional properties. In 1957 he took the enterprise public as Capital Cities Television Corporation.

Whereupon all hell broke loose. Television, in those very years, was crossing the line from being an intriguing novelty, a gizmo, to something that people just couldn't live without. Families without sets had become a pitiable minority in 1954, and by the end of the decade nine households out of ten were equipped with a tube. Advertisers, moreover, were discovering that the American public, all sensible arguments to the contrary notwithstanding, *believed* what they saw on television. Suddenly everybody from Du Pont to Vegematic was hot to purchase air time. You *had* to purchase air time, because there were really only two kinds of companies in America in the later 1950s: those that sponsored TV shows and those that didn't. The ones that did had names that everybody, from Grandpa down to little Johnny, recognized; the ones that didn't were lumped together under the ignominious rubric Brand X. Cigarettes, constipation remedies, drain unstuffers, nasal spray—if it was for sale in America, it was being hawked on television, and companies like Cap Cities, which had got in early and bought the airwaves for a song, found themselves selling seconds for what a minute used to cost, selling prime-time minutes for what it used to cost to run the station for a day.

Awash in money, Frank Smith went out and bought more airwaves, moving quickly but avoiding the high-priced scramble for the major metropolitan areas. By the middle sixties Cap Cities owned as many TV stations as the FCC allowed, and only then began the process of trading up into bigger, more lucrative markets. The outfit expanded its holdings in radio, was preparing to enter the publishing business, and had got itself listed on the Big Board. As of '65 the company was worth $60 million, and Tom Murphy, as Frank Smith's number-two and protégé, was pulling down a comfy $95,000 in salary, plus a package of stock options. Then, in 1966, the oracular Smitty, with the impeccable timing of a benefactor out of Dickens, performed his final kindness toward Tom Murphy: he dropped dead, leaving the younger man chairman and CEO at the age of forty-one.

Under Murphy the company would develop a reputation for leanness and decentralization. Mostly, however, it would develop a reputation for not having a reputation. In the high-visibility communications field, Murphy would manage to maintain the lowest of profiles. His style was the very opposite of the razzmatazz industry norm, and the absence of flamboyance made it easy to overlook the fact that, in deed if not in word, Murphy was, as *Advertising Age* columnist James Brady would point out in 1985, "every bit as acquisitive and ambitious as Rupert Murdoch and Si Newhouse."

As of the beginning of '85, Cap Cities' properties included nineteen television and radio stations, ten daily newspapers and twenty-seven weeklies, thirty-five trade periodicals, including the flagship *Women's Wear Daily* (part of Fairchild Publications, which Cap Cities swallowed whole in 1968), two electronic data-base operations, and fifty-five cable stations in sixteen states. The company's 1984 revenues had been $940 million, and its profits were over $140 million. Over the long term Cap Cities had performed fabulously well: investors who'd bought into the company at the time of the first public offering had improved their holdings by a factor of two hundred. The original shareholders, of whom Murphy himself was one, had bettered that by an undisclosed but significant multiple. An overall return on investment of 10,000/1 is a not unreasonable estimate. The chairman's holdings as of early 1985 were worth nearly $30 million.

Still, at that juncture Tom Murphy had a problem. In the vault was a big pile of corporate money—around 300 mil in cash— and the pile was gathering dust. For several years there'd been nothing around worth spending it on. Along with other media bigs, Murphy had been leaning on the FCC to raise the number of TV stations a single company could own; the FCC moved at the typical government pace, and though change would come in 1986, Murphy's hands had been tied in the meantime. Radio stations had come to seem nickel-dime. The cost of print properties had been inflated almost to the size of the egos of the people who were scarfing them up. Still, sitting on money was a bad idea; idle money made a company gouty. It was getting to be a big problem and it called for a big solution.

So Tom Murphy quietly and methodically went out and raised a couple billion dollars and announced one day that he was buying ABC. Nobody—not the Wall Street rumor mills nor the media themselves—seemed to know the slightest thing about it until it happened.

The news hit on March 19, 1985. It was the lead story in *The New York Times,* front page in the *Wall Street Journal,* and the top headline on everybody's evening news. The $3.5 billion takeover could only be talked about in terms of superlatives and firsts. It was the largest acquisition in history, outside of the oil business. It was the first time a television network had ever changed hands, a transaction that had previously been considered unthinkable. It was a deal that spun off consequences and conjectures ranging from the fate of "Monday Night Football" right on up to the future of the First Amendment. Media stocks soared as, all of a sudden, everybody agreed that they'd been undervalued all these years. Jesse Helms was making a move for CBS. Ted Turner would make a move for CBS. Journalists found themselves discussing the issue of network bosses' moral fiber, and social critics worried aloud about the increasing concentration of media control in the hands of giant corporations that were businesses first, communicators second. In its implications both financial and political, the ABC takeover seemed certain to stand as one of the pivotal business events of the last quarter of the twentieth century.

"But here's the funny part," says Tom Murphy, locking his hands behind his head, flicking his eyes in this owlish way he has, and telescoping all the way back to 1954. "There were lots of reasons why I shouldn't have taken that job from Frank Smith in the first place, and I almost *didn't* take it. I was on a good track at Lever Brothers and, in theory at least, I might have done just fine there—and with a lot less diciness and trouble. So OK, today I look smart for taking the five-year long shot and getting into an industry that went through the roof. But that basically had to do with being young, a little restless, and incredibly lucky in having a boss who was a lot smarter than I was. *He's* the one who made the prophecy about broadcasting."

Murphy's company, as it happens, is headquartered just around the corner from Lever House, and still occupies an erstwhile ecclesiastic residence; only now it's in the Villard Houses, formerly an adjunct to St. Patrick's Cathedral, today a New York City landmark whose courtyard provides the entrance to the Helmsley Palace Hotel. The chairman of Capital Cities–ABC presides over the top floor of the townhouse, in a setting that is less like a conventional office than a Georgian drawing room, with oak wainscoting, Oriental rugs, and wing chairs arranged in conversational groupings.

"You know," says Murphy, "one of the things the Business School can't teach you is what's a good business to get into at a given time—where the real growth is going to be. That's instinct—even if it's just instinct about whose advice you'll believe, out of all the advice that gets thrown at you. I might just as easily have picked, say, railroads, and been the world's greatest unsung manager in a company that was destined to go down the tubes no matter who was running it. For me, the whole thing started with the decision to take a chance on a guy with an idea."

That decision, however, didn't come out of nowhere. It had its context in the American Postwar Code, an ethos which held that you were wimping out unless you made a suitably stylish grab at the dangling brass ring, and which still reserved a place of at least secondary honor for the noble failure. A large-scale flop at the fringe of the known—that had some panache to it, that made for conversation. Whereas, middle-way success in the insulated belly of the already established—that seemed bourgeois even to the bourgeoisie. Plenty of guys would take that middle road, of course, and more than a few would saunter to the top along its gently graded slopes; but they were not the men who'd do the very best nor who would be best thought of. A certain taint of meekness, of spirit-mediocrity almost, would dog their reputations always.

Which (getting slightly ahead of ourselves) is precisely the complaint that some '49ers level against more recent entrants into business.

"These twenty-four-, twenty-six-, twenty-eight-year-olds today," says Peter McColough, chairman of Xerox Corporation—"I don't know what's with 'em. They're much more conservative than we were, and I don't even think they realize it. They seem to think that if you're playing it safe, that means you're being mature. I don't know if they're still reacting against the sixties or what, but they don't seem to have it in them to take the big chance. They just want to find a cozy little niche in something that's already been shown to work. Which isn't only deadly to the entrepreneurial spirit, but even in purely selfish terms it cuts way down on their chances for the big score. They have a much more narrowly constricted vision than we did of what constitutes a good job."

When McColough started out, he seemed to have *no* vision of what a good job was. Giving him the benefit of the doubt, he took the no-longer-fashionable, vaguely Zen approach of drifting toward the gravy with a minimum of will but a maximum of attentiveness. Either that, or he just plain didn't have a clue as to what he wanted.

Prior to attending the Business School, he'd studied law in his native Canada, passed that nation's bar, and flirted with the idea of a practice. He ended up deciding that corporate law had less to do with jurisprudence than with business, and really wasn't terribly exciting anyway, so he might as well bag it and get himself an MBA. At Harvard he was an undistinguished scholar, and in fact is remembered as part of a cadre who occasionally toted water pistols to class. But there is more to success in business than mere deftness at the case method, and McColough had two not inconsiderable advantages over the great majority of his classmates. One was his marvelously resonant *basso* voice, a voice that could have done the God part in *The Ten Commandments;* forget what he actually said, McColough held sway in class discussions by the sheer splendor of his tone. His other trump card was that already, in his middle twenties, he was going bald. His receding hair seemed not to consist of discrete strands but to constitute a translucent veil-like smudge on top of his large and squarish head, and this gave McColough an aura of gravity, authority, and certainty that took in all except those who knew him well. Those who knew him less well kept offering McColough the wrong jobs, and McColough kept taking them.

His first employment after Business School was as a chemical salesman with a firm up in Ottawa. There were only three things wrong with this job: the product, the position, and the location. So McColough ditched it and went to the Lehigh Coal and Navigation Company, in Philadelphia, as vice-president of sales. This was somewhat better; but only somewhat. He was closer to the action, and his big voice, balding pate, and one-two punch of MBA and law degree were earning him comfortably more than the Class average. Still, coal and barges, even as of 1950, were mature industries whose futures figured to be about as exciting as a slow leak. McColough hadn't chucked the practice of law and become an expatriate just to preside over some fat but eroding enterprise. He'd come to play, and he went back to the headhunters for something a little jazzier this time, something that would keep the juices flowing.

He was steered, in 1954, to a company called Haloid, a floundering concern whose very name was vaguely irritating, and in which he had no interest whatsoever. The only reason he agreed to visit the company at all—in balmy Rochester, no less—was that he didn't want to alienate the recruiter who'd suggested it. Maybe the guy would have a good idea next time.

So McColough headed north and was given the tour of the plant. He examined Haloid's primitive duplicating equipment and "was most unimpressed with it." It made images that looked like soft charcoal on moist toilet paper; mimeograph sheets were crisp as etchings by comparison. Clearly, this was a company going nowhere, and McColough, always a tactful sort, began preparing in his mind that most delicate of speeches, saying thanks-but-no-thanks to a good-hearted bunch of well-intentioned losers. What would have made the speech a little easier to say was that Haloid was actually asking him to take a 50-percent pay cut from his present job. True, they were offering an almost embarrassingly generous package of stock and options as well—but stock in *Haloid*? It was like being paid off in war bonds of a defeated nation.

On the other hand, if it was the big score that held

your interest, and if you had something of a gambler's turn of mind to begin with, you knew that salary was not the way to go; the way to go was to own a chunk of something. Joe Wilson, Haloid's president, was asking McColough to sign on for five years. Five years *always* seemed to be the trial period back in those days of less than instant gratification; it was the same five years whether you were a capitalist manager or a Soviet farmer, and it was followed by the same agonizing reappraisal of where the experiment had got you. The suspense, if it didn't drive you nuts, was very sexy. McColough came aboard.

In 1956 Haloid started working on the first plain-paper copier, the 914, and also started wondering how, with its puny resources, it was going to get the damn thing manufactured and distributed. There ensued a Great Moment in Market Research. IBM, having got wind of what was going on in Rochester, suggested that maybe *they* should handle the making and marketing of the new machines, in return for a slice of the proceeds. This, in principle, was dandy with the folks at Haloid; in fact, it spelled salvation. But IBM, legendary for its circumspection, wasn't about to jump in cold, without a feasibility study, and they hired the top-drawer consulting firm of Arthur D. Little to run one. Many thousands of dollars later the team of experts hunkered down over their clipboards and somberly reported that a gadget for making copies was a cute idea, but that it cost too much and not that many people really needed it. IBM, on second thought, would not be showing up for the wedding. Peter McColough lost hair over that one.

So imagine you're Haloid and the most competent people in the country, people *famous* for being smart, have just told you that your new invention is a turkey, a bow-wow, an Edsel. What do you do? "You get depressed," McColough says. "But we went ahead anyway. This wasn't courage or vision necessarily. We just didn't have a choice.

"Look," he goes on, "these days people have a hard time understanding this sort of rashness, but for seven or eight years—seven or eight years straight!—Haloid had been spending more on research and development than they'd been earning. That is a policy of what you might call confident desperation, and what it meant, very simply, is that we were betting the company—buildings, jobs, trays in the cafeteria—on that product. The whole wad was on the table. No 914, no Haloid, period."

The rest of the story has been often cited. When the 914 was released in 1960, it was not sold, but rented, in accordance with a marketing scheme developed in part by Peter McColough himself (and not taken into account by IBM's consultants). The launch was one of the most successful new-product introductions in history, and an absolutely seminal event in the emergence of the information age. Haloid became Xerox, sales grew at an exophthalmic 30 percent a year through the sixties and into the seventies, and the stock was such a Wall Street darling that its price-to-earnings ratio reached a slightly comical eighty-eight. You couldn't overvalue Xerox. Xerox had invented the biggest growth industry in the world, and it owned that industry cold. Xerox was everything bold, smart, solid yet supple about how business was done in the big time.

Or so it seemed for a while. Then Xerox started making mistakes; large ones. In 1969, itchy to get into the computer business, they bought a mainframe company called

Scientific Data Systems, Inc., for just shy of a billion dollars. They paid too much for it, they didn't know how to make it go, and it was the wrong part of the industry to invest in to begin with; they tanked it as an $84 million write-off after running divisional losses every quarter for six straight years. Meanwhile, after a series of patent battles, the company kissed its virtual monopoly in copiers goodbye, as Kodak, IBM, a slew of smaller U.S. companies, and of course the Japanese all went in for "xeroxing." So McColough's outfit moved to cover its bets by going after a chunk of the electronic-typewriter action. They went into that game too late, with a machine that cost too much and was obsolescent almost before it rolled out the door. In 1975, for the first time in its history, Xerox posted a drop in earnings. By 1978 the business press was saying rather ungallant things about its former sweetheart, parodying the company's thunderous ineffectiveness by likening Pete McColough to "the bereft King Lear, threatening, 'I will do such things—what they are yet I know not—but they shall be the terrors of the earth.' "*

McColough, who became Xerox's president in 1966, CEO in '68, and chairman in '71, has borne the biggest share of the blame for the company's downturn, and there is no question that some of his decisions have been inscrutable. The specific blunders, though, really aren't very interesting; they're mainly garden-variety miscalculations and mis-timings inflated to heroic scale. The interesting part is the rhythm they fall into. Back in the days of "confident desperation," Xerox seemed to do everything on a hunch, and everything right. It left the luxury of careful

---

* "Xerox Is Trying Too Hard," *Fortune*, March 13, 1978.

circumspection to companies that could afford it, like IBM. By the middle sixties, though, Xerox, too, was cautious— and never more so than when spending vast sums on defensive acquisitions. There were reactive moves that Xerox couldn't afford not to make, but it had essentially stopped initiating anything. The stakes *should* have seemed lower, now that survival was secure; but the sheer ballooning scale of things made the ante seem paralyzingly expensive. Prestige, image, the tentative affection of Wall Street and the hard-won loyalty of stockholders—the company had all those things to lose, and nothing left to gain but more of the same. It had become an institution, and it moved with the heavy splendor of an ocean liner through waters treacherous with speedboats and subs.

History is oddly sporting about such things. It builds up empires and massive fortunes, yet retains a soft spot for the underdog, and allows to the outsider certain stratagems, a certain mobility, and even a certain ruthlessness that the biggest, strongest companies or nations are barred by their positions from employing. Xerox was coming to realize that by the beginning of the seventies. As it happened, American business generally was being taught about the same lesson at about the same time. And everybody seemed surprised by what was going on, as if it had never, ever happened before.

five

The Long Honeymoon

In 1952, Gary Cooper won an Oscar for *High Noon,* Stan "the Man" Musial copped the National League batting title, and a cement dealer from Chicago went out and bought the Empire State Building.

Henry Crown had wanted to buy the 102-story skyscraper when it first came up for sale the year before, but he'd been stymied; a syndicate had already been put together, and he could only get in for a measly 23 percent. So he bought his shares and bided his time.

Then one day he called his acquaintance Robert Young, chairman and leading shareholder of the Chesapeake and Ohio Railroad, who owned another 23 percent. "Bob," he said, "I don't see that it does either one of us a damn bit of good to own a quarter of the thing. Whaddya say I buy you out?"

"Whaddya say I buy *you* out?" countered Young.

They resolved the matter by a multimillion-dollar variant of the I-cut-you-choose method by which two kids divvy up a piece of cake. Crown named a price, and Young then had the option of either buying or selling at the figure. He asked for a day to think it over. Then he called Crown back.

"Congratulations, Henry," he said. "You bought it."

In short order, the other, smaller investors also sold out to Crown, leaving him the sole owner of the most famous building in the New World, the Chartres of American enterprise.

"So you'll excuse me," says Lester Crown, Henry's son and a graduate of Harvard B School, Class of '49, "if I came of age believing that there weren't any built-in limits, that there wasn't anywhere that the snowball had to stop. As of the 1950s, it really seemed that anything at all was possible.

"Not," he goes on, "that my father started out in life with zero. He started out *below* zero. *His* father came over from Latvia and worked in a sweatshop making suspenders. When my father was a boy, if he wanted a sweet roll, he worked for the money, then bought the roll instead of taking the streetcar. You want Horatio Alger? I'm giving you Horatio Alger."

He tells a good story, Lester Crown does, punchy and wry, though with just a hint of reluctance in his voice, a slight glitch in his timing, as if from the long habit of watching his father out of the corner of his eye and wondering if it was yet his turn to speak. Sixty years old, looking younger, he is still the son, the inheritor. In a sense, all the men of '49 were heirs, beneficiaries of the moment when the decades of laying the groundwork for American preeminence were about to be fulfilled. For Lester Crown, though, the whole edifice, not just the foundation, had already been put in place. The gritty work of getting the dynasty established had been done back in the days when management was a profession only in the sense that, say, bareknuckle boxing was a profession. When Lester Crown was sent to Harvard, it was to be trained not in the grubby processes of amassing wealth, but in the more dignified though less authoritative skills of husbanding the billion-dollar family fortune and of exercising the familial clout with suitable discretion.

Back in 1919, things had been a little different. That year Henry Crown scraped together $10,000 and launched a piddling little sand-and-gravel operation called the Material Service Company. The company was in Chicago, and practically from day one it started winning municipal contracts. Practically from day two, allegations of unsanitary dealings with City Hall started flying.* Nothing was ever proved, and the Material Service barges and buggies kept hauling the stone. It was a business that called for a lot of improvising. When it was time to negotiate a labor contract, the teamster bosses would come to the Crown home, put their guns down on the kitchen table, and if they were happy with the management offer, they'd accept a glass of tea from Mrs. Crown. Strategic planning consisted of making damn sure that somehow or other you got title to a quarry that was closer to the construction site than the other guy's. It was basic but it worked. By 1958 Material Service was worth so much money that when Crown Se-

---

* Allegations about the Crowns' companies' business procedures have never *stopped* flying. See pages 183–186.

nior folded it into the mammoth defense contractor General Dynamics, his main motivation was that he needed a personal bank. The merger made him GD's largest stockholder, with just shy of ten million shares worth around $650 million. Along the way, Crown had also come to own pieces of Hilton Hotels, Aetna Life and Casualty, Pennzoil, and Trans World Airlines, as well as real estate in Chicago, New York, and California.

"My father managed to do well in every decade, in every sort of economy," says Lester Crown. "He always found a way—buying, selling, trading, waiting. But the fifties and the sixties—even he had to pinch himself about how good things were back then, how easy it all seemed. That was a dream time. Those were the classical days."

They were the days in which success was becoming the rule and not the exception in America, in which it seemed possible to have far more winners than losers. Between 1950 and 1960 the gross national product nearly doubled; in the next decade it nearly doubled again. Disposable income, in constant dollars, was increasing by an average of almost 5 percent a year. Those were the days when it was starting to seem nothing more than obvious that next year's car would be bigger than this year's, with more chrome on it, and tinted glass, and that while the first house a couple bought might be only a nest, it would be followed soon by a three-bedroom split-level, then followed again by the stately Cape they'd always really wanted.

"You could produce cheap," remembers Crown. "You could sell everything you had, and there were always more orders waiting. The only limit was your guts in going out to borrow money to build more plant to make things big ger. The only guys who got hurt were the guys who didn't believe, who played it close to the vest because they just couldn't conceive of things staying this good for this long; it cost them, that lack of faith—they got swallowed up.

"But we believed, we built. Whatever was going on, we were going to bet on it in a big way—bigger than the Harvard Business School would have called prudent, I expect. Aerospace was booming, and GD looked golden at the time. Construction—forget it; you barely had time to overhaul the trucks before they had to be out on another job. People were starting to fly like crazy, and the hotel business was phenomenal. Freight was moving, and even the railroads were hanging in. The banks, the insurance companies couldn't make a bad investment.

"Everything was working and everything fit together. It was a dream time, believe me. But you know what happened after a while? People stopped pinching themselves, stopped knocking on wood. People go to extremes, have you ever noticed? First they can't believe that things will stay this good till Tuesday, then they go exactly the opposite and act like things will stay this good forever."

Things didn't. Still, the fifties and the sixties in America were the longest and most luscious honeymoon that the modern world had ever seen.

In the ˙20 months between 1950 and 1960 the economy advanced in all but four, creating over eight million new jobs along the way and nearly doubling the total dollars paid to employees. By 1960 the momentum had become so enormous that there began a roll of over four years in which the economy outperformed its previous monthly record *every single month*. Neither the Cuban missile crisis, nor the assassination of John F. Kennedy, nor the first wave of urban riots could scotch the streak. By 1964 Americans were paying for the squalid necessities of food, clothing, and shelter with only 48 percent of their collective income, and the national mood had become so blithe that 46 percent of the population believed there would never again be even a mild recession. By the middle sixties nearly fifteen million overnourished citizens had joined the Metrecal-for-lunch bunch. The prosperity extended to every region, every state, and every industry that the government bothered to monitor. From manufacturing to finance to commercial fishing to picking up the garbage, every sector, like biscuits rising in the same warm oven, was turning golden.

It was hard to make a bad move, either professional or geographical, in those days. A '49er named Don Frisbee headed for Oregon, a part of the world whose existence had barely been alluded to at Harvard, and ended up as chairman of Pacific Power and Light. A guy named Frank Mayers, after a youthful misadventure trying to market a laxative called Prunex, took the straight and narrow road to the chairmanship of Bristol-Myers. Not that you had to go ultra-mainstream to cash in on the promise of the long honeymoon. With everybody traveling, billions of dollars were suddenly being left, quite literally, at the side of the road, and '49ers jumped in among the earliest investors in Holiday Inns and Tastee-Freezes. The hamburger with all the trimmings was being fried, grilled, and broiled into history, and '49er John Walker was abetting the process as president of Mount Olive Pickle Company, Mount Olive, North Carolina.

Still, even though almost everyone was doing fine,

there were certain guys and certain careers that stood out as being most perfectly wedded to their context, most perfectly in harmony with their place and time. And no career suggests the nuances of the long honeymoon better than that of Marvin Traub, chairman of Bloomingdale's. Traub's star and the American living standard rose as one, as shopping became the nation's favorite participant sport.

Marvin Traub grew up in a household obsessed with ladies' lingerie. Bras and girdles, girdles and bras—that's all the Traubs ever seemed to talk about at the dinner table. Spandex, fiber-fill, underwires, the relative appeal of black or flesh-toned panties—little Marvin was immersed in it every evening, and he took on a rather precociously somber aspect, a bit severe around the mouth, slightly shadowed under the eyes. No wonder—he was burdened with great secrets: he knew more about what went on beneath a woman's dress than any other twelve-year-old in the city of New York.

His father was a vice-president of the lingerie company Lily of France, his mother was a fashion director for Bonwit Teller. Family friends tended to hail from the upper echelons of the department-store industry. When Traub applied to Harvard College to do his undergraduate work, his application was accompanied by a letter of reference from Stanley Marcus, as in Neiman-Marcus. When he got out of the service and was plotting his next move, he went for advice to another "uncle," Jack Straus, a scion of one of the clans that founded Macy's. Straus tried to talk Traub out of bothering with business school—what could these stiffs teach you in a classroom that you couldn't learn quicker and better on the selling floor? But Traub was a studious type. At the Business School, in fact, he and his two best friends would come to be dubbed the Three Wise Men. Traub and Sumner Feldberg, chairman of Zayre stores, and Wilbur Cowett, an independent financial consultant in New York—they'd studied humanities together as undergraduates and they'd held on to the undergraduate habit of impassioned discussions that went on long into the night. It was rumored they read books that weren't on the syllabi. Occasionally they'd cite Hobbes or Hegel in class, and other guys would roll their eyes.

Upon graduation, Traub joined up with Alexander's, a downmarket department store where even the mannequins looked like their clothing itched behind the knees. Within a year, however, he'd made his move and signed on with the outfit he was born to run. This was 1950. A lot of people were jumping the gun and calling it the first year of the second half of the century, and while their arithmetic was cockeyed, in some ways they were right. In 1950 the future seemed cozy as an egg, and someone on high seemed to be looking out for Marvin Traub. He was groomed with unfailing care, eased through seven different jobs in seven years, getting on terms with every niche and alcove of the premises. They stuck him in the basement, yanked him up to housewares, zipped him through the short course in linens and in food, gave him the refresher, even, in bras and girdles. In 1956, when he was only thirty-one, he was made a merchandise manager.

And not just *any* merchandise manager, but merchandise manager in the hottest part of the store: Home Furnishings. Home Furnishings laid out model rooms delineated by Masonite partitions, and the successive rooms, like frames in a comic strip, became vignettes of modern life. They were filled with furniture in the Scandinavian backache style, all blond wood and bruising edges, and with hovering lamps that seemed inspired by the beacons that dangle over dentists' chairs. Home Furnishings was crucial in 1956 because it was the spearhead of an image-change that Bloomie's was just then undergoing, from working-class and practical to upper-middle and chic. Bloomingdale's, you see, hadn't always been a fancy store, any more than America had always been a fancy country. They'd both started out, in fact, rather on the austere and maybe even the ascetic side.

Bloomie's had opened its doors way back in 1872, and it was anything but glitzy at the time. It was a small dry-goods emporium selling corsets, millinery, hoopskirts, gloves, and undies; the scale of the enterprise was such that its gross receipts for the first full day of business came to $3.68. The original store was located at Third Avenue and 56th Street, and this in itself marked the establishment as marginal: the fashionable part of Manhattan back then was Union Square. The upper east side was where the hired help lived, a demimonde of tenements, fire escapes, and laundry flapping in the ersatz breeze created by the Third Avenue El. Central Park was just then being built, was still a jumble of marshes and half-reclaimed pastures, and who wanted to live near a swamp?

By the 1920s the city had moved uptown to meet the store, and Bloomie's was a resounding success—though still in a thoroughly unglamorous, Sears, Roebuck sort of way. It had moved to its present location—the entire square block between 59th and 60th Streets and Third and Lexington Avenues—and when, in 1926, the company went public, its stock was deemed attractive enough so that the entire offering was gobbled up by ten a.m. of the first day it was available. By 1945 Bloomie's annual sales had burgeoned to more than $44 million.

Yet, up to that time the growth had been gradual, linear; the store's fundamental philosophy, like the nation's bedrock Calvinist assumptions, hadn't really changed. America was a place where people lived, worked, went to church and occasionally the movies, and died, and Bloomingdale's was a facility that provided things those people *needed*. After World War II, however, with the vets having seen Paree and the peacetime economy warming up and the second Jazz Age starting to jitterbug, that grayly virtuous Puritan approach to life and retailing no longer seemed quite good enough, had somehow come to seem archaic. There were limits, after all, to what human beings actually required, how many pairs of socks, say, they'd go through in a year. On the other hand, given human imagination and the miracle of spiraling disposable income, there were virtually limitless horizons for what people could be induced to *crave*, for "needs" that a savvy merchant might not just serve, but cozen into being.

And that's where Marvin Traub came in. He was a new man for a new day, not just another seat-of-the-pants merchandiser, but a certifiable Ivy League maven. He had the sophistication to understand the value of publicity, and the polish to get out there and whip some up. He had the lessons of Ad Prac to help him in dealing with recalcitrant suppliers, making sure that Bloomie's got the stuff that no one else could offer. Most of all, Harvard Business School had taught him to think supremely big: was there any reason that a department store couldn't be GM, couldn't be the phone company? Traub was a man steamrolling right over predigested wisdom as to limits, and getting rid of limits was exactly what the long honeymoon was all about.

"What we were trying to do back in the fifties and the sixties," he recalls, speaking from the chairman's office he's occupied since 1978—an office on Bloomingdale's top floor, insulated from the buzz of traffic and the almost lubricious mood the store engenders in its habitués— "is figure out the trends in our country and stay ahead of them."

In this they succeeded to a degree suggestive almost of the Faustian. Traub and company sensed the precise historical moment when status in America was coming to be seen in terms of the indulgence of a vague and endlessly manipulable quality called taste. Taste was ethereal, it applied to everything, and you could never have too much of it, or too many of the things in which it cloaked itself. Pricey French-milled soaps in the shape of bell peppers and Bartlett pears—why not? Crystal decanters equipped with septa for holding four different-colored liqueurs—no home should be without one. Though taste, of course, could be revised at any moment and found its purest expression in things that served no purpose whatsoever, as in arrangements of steel balls on strings that proved, over and over again, certain basic principles of Newtonian mechanics. From electric can-openers to tab collars to infrared lamps for tanning at home, if it was new, if it was shiny, Bloomie's was in the forefront in getting it promoted, in teaching the native to want it.

The native they were dealing with was a consumer who'd never had it so good. In the immediate postwar

years, homes were being slapped up at an utterly unprecedented pace, and by 1954, 58 percent of all Americans
held title to their dwellings. Having roofs over their heads,
the young marrieds—including the prolific '49ers, who
would average 3.1 kids per man—started reproducing at a
record clip. In '54, babies were spilling out to the tune of
eleven thousand a day. These were the kids who would become the Me Generation—and who could really blame
them? They became what they beheld. They were emerg-
ing into a world where they'd all have their very own red
wagons and trikes and bikes, and later on their very own
Mustangs and Camaros to ride around the smooth suburban streets. They'd have their own TV sets, their own prin-
cess telephones, they'd have clean new schools with virgin
textbooks whose spines would crackle the first time they
were opened. Bloomingdale's would sell them spanking-
new outfits for every Christmas and every Easter, there'd
be flouncy-bouncy canopy beds for the girls and gas-
powered planes that flew around in circles for the boys.

Nor would these indulgences be only for the young.
Grownups, too, were learning how to play; by the end of
the fifties, the leisured classes had become the leisured
masses. "You could always sell ties," says Marvin Traub,
"but now you could sell sailing equipment, elaborate bar-
becues and other things going with a new leisure life-
style." In 1959 six times as many Americans were enrolled
in ballroom-dancing classes as in colleges and universities.
Florida's sport-fishing industry was worth more than its
citrus crop. Georgia's tourist trade brought in more money
than King Cotton. In California more boats were being
sold than cars, and in New York State on July Fourth
weekend, more people drowned than murdered themselves

on the highways. As much money was spent on dogs that year as on lawyers. As of 1960 the U.S. boasted a quarter-million swimming pools, up more than 2,000 percent from 1950, and the national tab for inflatable rafts and rubber duckies stood at $40 million. In 1964 American women spent half again as much in beauty parlors as the government of Switzerland shelled out to run its country.

In an atmosphere like that, Bloomingdale's was absolutely on the mark in hawking battery-powered swizzle sticks and gold-plated fixtures for the john, paving the way for the slightly later phenomena of the paper bathing suit, the forty-dollar *après*-sun emollient, the double-figure chunk of cheese. It was right, too, in making its window displays increasingly expressionistic, increasingly surreal, as if the goodies being offered for sale existed in no context whatsoever, neither moral nor historical nor even esthetic, but floated unencumbered in some empyrean of affluence utterly devoid of complicating values.

By the end of the 1960s, Bloomingdale's sales had burgeoned to $192 million, five satellite stores had cropped up in the suburbs, and Marvin Traub, for his part in the heyday, had been made president of the company at the age of forty-four. The two decades that led up to his election had been, in truth, the classical period for buying and selling in America. But the thing about classical times is that they have a way of leading seamlessly on toward decadent ones, and at some point, though the precise moment remains elusive, the shadow line, it seems in retrospect, had already been irreversibly crossed.

Had it been crossed as early as the late fifties, when Marvin Traub started leading coveys of buyers around Europe, piecing together facsimiles of bedrooms from seventeenth-century Dutch paintings or of the King of Naples' gazebo? When exotic trinkets started finding their way to Bloomingdale's as ineluctably as they'd landed in the British Museum during *that* nation's imperial moment? Had it happened in 1960, when the theme promotions began, when Bloomie's started hyping the exportable treasure of entire foreign nations? (No one seemed concerned, in those euphoric days, about fostering in the American consumer a too quick appetite for imported goods.) First had come Italy. Twenty buyers, following in Traub's wake, swarmed all over that country and came back with furniture, with textiles, with hunks of Pompeiian lava, with *Italians*. They brought musicians with Tyrolean hats, and baffled artisans who sucked their teeth while trying to carve tiles right there on the selling floor. The next year it was France, complete with a re-creation of the entire Rue Faubourg St. Honoré. One year they built a whole Thai house in the middle of the store and called the extravaganza "The King and I." In 1966, macabre but true, the theme was "The Color of Southeast Asia."

It was great spectacle, all of this. It was marketing *chutzpah* carried far beyond the most grandiose tales from the HBS casebook, and the wealthy new America gobbled it up and carried it happily home in those famous Bloomingdale's shopping bags—the shopping bags that, as Marvin Traub observes, "some people think of as matched luggage."

But what, in the meantime, was happening to that *other* America—the America whose scrappy, stoic energy was what had built this fancier, more decorative version in the first place? Where was the lean, austere America of GI Bill moxie, of rolled-up workshirt sleeves, of indulgence deferred in the name of service—the America that had spawned the men of '49 and whose banner they were carrying? That America was already fading, and the men of the postwar, by their very success, were helping it to fade. Back in '47 they'd thrown themselves against the gates of Harvard Business School, clamoring with an exigent ambition to make things better than they'd ever been. Both the good news and the bad were contained in the fact that they'd done what they set out to do.

"We have grown soft," chided John F. Kennedy, making his run for the Presidency in 1959—"physically, mentally, spiritually soft." The sense of national mission, Kennedy warned, had been steadily eroding, the national will was growing ever more lethargic. That there would be a comeuppance was as safe a bet as death and taxes. "The slow corrosion of luxury," said the Senator from Massachusetts, "is already beginning to show."

Tens of millions of people voted for Kennedy. Some even went on fifty-mile hikes on his advice. But they didn't seem inclined to let his drear admonitory message get beneath their skin. Once the speech was over and the goose bumps had subsided, common sense prevailed and people reassured themselves that the whole to-do was only politics. And maybe it was. But as politics goes, it wasn't bad as prophecy.

"Yup," says Lester Crown, "those were some pretty fantastic years. Then at some point the years were less fantastic. They were still pretty damn good, but suddenly things seemed complicated, suddenly there were problems."

Crown pauses, puts his palms flat on his desk, glances rather absently around his office. His official title is chairman of Material Service, now a half-billion-dollar-plus division of General Dynamics; he's also an executive vice-president of the parent corporation, as well as the most powerful member of its board. He deals routinely with the top echelons of the Pentagon and, less routinely, with Congressional committees looking into malfeasances in defense-related billings. He is a partner of George Steinbrenner in ownership of the New York Yankees, and he also holds pieces of the St. Louis Blues and the Chicago Bulls. For all that, his office bears the unmistakable stamp of the family operation. It's not a place for impressing outsiders or making clients feel important. The paneling is the sort that comes in 4 x 8 sheets, and on it is hung not original art or signed lithographs, but snapshots of Crown's seven kids and of his wife. When he resumes, he seems almost to be talking to the photos.

"The balloon started coming back down. Inflation was all of a sudden a major problem. Foreign competition was suddenly no joke. There were shortages here and there that took us unawares.

"So what are you asking me?" he says, though no question has been asked. "Are you asking me if we were the guys who were supposed to be smart, so shrewd, with such good eyes that we should've seen those things coming and battled them off?

"If that's what you're asking me," he says, "I really couldn't tell you."

Interlude

What Becomes
a Legend Most?
I

Stanley Greenfield had held on to his proclivity for taking
charge of things, and in 1959, in his then role of Class Secretary, he was presiding as master of ceremonies at his
Class's tenth reunion. He moved to the lectern in the cav-
ernous lecture hall of Baker Library, told his colleagues to
put away their family snapshots so he could make a few
announcements, and proceeded to say it gave him great
pleasure to inform them that the Class of '49, only a decade out of Business School, already boasted twenty-nine
guys who were worth a million bucks.

A murmur of approval hummed through the room,
punctuated here and there by pockets of applause. Then,
from near the back, came a voice that refused to be impressed. "Who's been pissing it away?" it asked. "We had
thirty-two when we started."

The number may have been fanciful, but the point and
its unspoken implications were hard to argue. If the Class
of '49 was looking for things to congratulate itself about, it
would have to look farther than mere wealth, because the
Class, collectively, had been rich before it ever set foot in
the marketplace.

The Class contained, for instance, an Indian prince
who had strode the campus regally unencumbered while a
servant padded silently behind, carrying his books and
bowing to members of the faculty, presuming to precede
his master only when there was a door to be opened or a
piece of litter to be lifted from his path; the prince's father,
thinking it unfitting for his heir to live among commoners,
had rented the top floor of a Boston hotel for his two-year
sojourn. The Class included, as well, Marc Wallenberg,
cousin of the mythic Raoul Wallenberg, famous for his rescue of European Jews, and a scion of the family that did
much of Sweden's banking; when Marc Wallenberg blew
his brains out some years later, for reasons not fiscal but
personal, a panic rocked the exchanges of Stockholm.
Claude Cartier, while at Business School, had dazzled his
classmates with his endless supply of cufflinks and the
dashing infrequency of his appearances at morning sem-
inars.

Among the homegrown, aside from brand-name sons
like Henderson and Crown, the class included Daniel
Parker, as in Parker Pen, who cruised the environs of Soldiers Field in a gleaming new Oldsmobile convertible, the
cost of which was a great subject of conjecture in those
days of lingering shortages and gray-market prices. The
cost of the whitewalls, at least, could have been pegged
pretty closely by classmate Gerry O'Neill, heir to a Mid-

western family outfit called General Tire and Rubber. Also on the roster were Jim Love, of the clan that had founded Burlington Mills, and Jim Weinberg, whose father, Sydney, was the guiding spirit of Goldman, Sachs, had been a close adviser of FDR, and may have set a record by sitting on no fewer than thirty-five corporate boards.

Wealth, then, was the easy part of the Class's achievement, and the part least convincing to take credit for. The dollar amounts made for entertaining scuttlebutt, but the Class of '49 seemed to be aiming higher. While still at Business School, they'd gone far beyond the usual class-pride hijinks and made an eight-millimeter epic about themselves; they called the film *Tomorrow's Leaders Today.* "It was a comedy," Stanley Greenfield would recall, "a joke—but let me tell you something: even then there were plenty of us who weren't laughing." The Class had surveyed itself on graduation and again in '54 and yet again at the ten-year mark, and it kept its archives neatly tabulated. Consciously or otherwise, the men of '49 seemed to be angling for a place in history. In essaying the giant leap from gossip into legend, though, they would have to find ways of disseminating their lore far beyond their own reunions. They'd somehow have to link their story with the story of the larger world around them.

By 1959, as it happened, that process was already under way. It had been set in motion five years previous, when Stanley Greenfield, never lacking in initiative, had spent a lot of time on the telephone with the editors of *Fortune,* trying to convince them to run a piece on the occasion of his Class's *fifth* reunion. An item in the business press—*that* would be a memorable coup for a Class Secretary to pull off, and Greenfield, who in those years had been working at *Look,* was no stranger to the mechanics of magazine flackery. You schmoozed, you cajoled, you called back again the following Monday, and if a little white space opened up between the ads, you might be able to generate some print. Felicitously, back in June of '54, a little white space had become available, and the Class of '49 began its media career with a brief notice entitled "Harvard Business Graduates—Five Years Out."

The funny part was that the item was published as a sidebar to a much longer article called "The Business Schools: Pass or Flunk?"—which was in the main a withering indictment of business education in America. In the boomtime stampede of young men seeking entree into commerce, the article maintained, far too many cynically conceived and badly staffed institutions were turning out far too many badly taught and utterly uncultivated functionaries who hadn't been that bright to begin with. In 1954 nearly 15 percent of all college students were majoring in business; their median IQ was lower than that of every other academic group except those who wore whistles around their necks and would someday be apostrophized as "Coach."

That was the bad news. The good news was largely contained in the half-page box which limned the progress of the Harvard B School Class of '49. As of 1954, the median class salary had risen to $8,300—just under thirty grand in 1982 money, double their real earnings of five years before. More than a third of the '49ers were still working for the companies that had first hired them, though a surprising 4.5 percent had been fired at one time or another. Still, only one class member was out of a job in 1954, and fortunately he was a millionaire. Fourteen percent were already in business for themselves, and fully six out of ten cockily predicted that they would be someday; in this, as in no other aspect of their shared ambitions, the Class would fall far short, and the failure would be tell-ing.* Still, by any measure the men of '49 were doing aw-fully well, and a role *vis-à-vis* the larger world was beginning to be defined for them: by example, they would demonstrate that business ambitions led on to fulfillment; they would help, just by being there, to keep the dream alive in others.

Moreover, since the habits and opinions of the Class of '49 were being recorded in mainstream print, those habits and opinions would loom disproportionately large in defin-ing what the mainstream was about. The fifties were the fifties, that is to say, because 80 percent of men like the '49ers were married and had fathered 1.3 children before they were thirty, because under 1 percent were separated or divorced as of that age, and if any were homosexual, the fact didn't get reported to *Fortune* magazine. Almost four '49ers in five had preferred the hardheaded Eisenhower to the eggheaded Stevenson in the 1952 election, and nine out of ten believed that world communism posed a serious threat to the United States. Two point seven percent of the '49ers had had ulcers since graduating, and 14.8 percent expected to end up with them before their working days were through; you sort of got the feeling that some '49ers actually *wanted* ulcers, because stress was morbidly fash-ionable in the fifties, and the telltale glass of milk in the company cafeteria or the bottle of Mylanta in the top desk

---

* See pages 105–123.

drawer could mark a young executive as a fellow on the move.

Thus the Class had been presented in 1954. In terms of the emergence of the '49er legend, however, the data themselves were far less important than the fact that the article had been printed at all. A cycle had been started. In future, the press would be all the more likely to trot out the '49ers for the simple reason that the press now had its very own notes to look back on. Logically, there was no compelling reason why 1948 or 1950 should not have claimed the place of honor as the epicenter of American optimism, drive, and conspicuous accomplishment. But 1949 had come in with the first installment in the ledger, and 1949 would be all but impossible to displace. When deadline journalism gets yellow at the edges, it starts to be called history.

Sure enough, in 1959 *Fortune* again turned its attention to the Class, and in no mere sidebar this time around. This time the men of that golden season rated nothing short of a brief sociological treatise. "Next to juvenile delinquents," the article began, "there is probably no group of Americans more earnestly discussed . . . than those suburbanites, most of them in their middle thirties, who help run the nation's corporations as junior executives." The '49ers were then introduced as "a very good, top-quality sample" of that group; their emblematic role, which had been left to inference in 1954, had now been made explicit.

"The $14,000-a-Year Man" is what the 1959 article was called, its title derived from what was then the '49ers' median salary. Equivalent to $49,000 in the debased coin of 1985, $14,000 was a figure to conjure with, a figure to sell magazines with, back then. Fourteen thou was enough to buy virtually all the things whose gleaming presence was the very stuff and essence of the long honeymoon. By the time they were ten years out of school, three quarters of the men of '49 were homeowners. One in twelve had managed to scrape together the down payment for a summer house as well, and 15 percent were already skippers of their own boats. As of 1959, the year that Cadillac apotheosized the tail fin with its loftily mounted bullet taillights, half the '49ers owned two or more cars.

Yet in that age of billowing expectations, the Harvard MBAs were not presented as exceptions, their standing was not portrayed as beyond the range of normal opportunity. Fifties revisionism notwithstanding, people *were* more alike back then, and the men of '49, Harvard or no Harvard, could honestly be served up as being like the average joe, only more so, a little further along on the shared road traveled by nearly everyone in an America not yet shocked and bamboozled into fragments.

Consensus was the key. That, and a half-conscious determination not to notice things that might disrupt consensus. As the following decades would develop a fetish for the fringes, so the fifties had a mania for the middle. The fringes existed, but they weren't seen to matter. Consider the treatment of the Beats, the period's most prophetic group of social critics. Someone slapped a Commie-sounding suffix onto them, everybody had a good derisive laugh out of it, and the whole phenomenon was neutralized in the bongo-tapping persona of Maynard G. Krebs. Societal rough edges were as unwelcome as cowlicks, and even among such an *ipso facto* mainstream group as the Class of '49 a certain flattening was to be seen in its preparation for public consumption. In the authorized version there was such a creature as a "typical" '49er. He flourished in a corporation of five thousand people. He believed in the tenets of his School and he was tickled he'd gone there. He was happy in his striving and thought of sober application as the height of virtue and of sanity itself.

In fact it wasn't quite that simple. Beneath the unruffled surface of the Class's public image, a fair amount of relative weirdness was to be found. A '49er named Warren McConihe, for example, remembered as a quiet, reclusive fellow, not the go-getter type at all, had one day, shortly after graduation, taken a cleaver to his mom, and was passing his time in an institution for the criminally deranged. Promising ad man Jack O'Connell had left his more conventional colleagues scratching their heads, by going off to produce, direct, coscript, and appear in a movie that touched on cohabitation and gender ambiguity and bore the ominous title *Greenwich Village Story*. John L. Cleveland, Jr., son of the chairman of Guaranty Trust Company, had kissed off the commercial life and settled into writing plays, surfacing now and again in such alternative locations as Vermont and Jackson Hole, Wyoming.

Nor was it universally true that the B School grads continued to embrace the B School way of doing things or that they invariably rode their education to corporate success. A fellow named Paul Hatch was showing himself far more adept at getting jobs than keeping them—he'd have had more than thirty-five before he was through—and was on his way to accumulating a stack of obsolete business cards thick as a pinochle deck; in later life he'd write a manual for the recently axed, entitled *I've Just Been Fired*.

Forty-niner Kirk Drumheller, meanwhile, who would end up as a solar-energy project manager for Batelle Northwest, was moving toward the conviction that "many of the problems of today's industry are a result of the permeation of the Harvard Business School philosophy of the '40s," and that "much of the change in our relative position of strength in the world results from the adoption of this philosophy."

Even among those '49ers who most closely approximated the "typical" there was beginning, by the end of the fifties, to be a quiet but somewhat nervous acknowledgment that the world was thornier and more bedeviling than it had seemed from Soldiers Field. At his tenth reunion the specimen '49er was thirty-six years old. His family was launched, his career was on track, and at roughly the midpoint of his life he had the ambivalent luxury of drawing practically the first contemplative, appraising breaths he'd had time for since Pearl Harbor. Looking around, he saw a world in which the comforting old certainties about Yankee superiority were already getting harder to maintain and in which the old gung-ho rhetoric was coming to sound as empty as a gutted fish. The Russians had already put up Sputnik, had already photographed the dark side of the moon, had already put a satellite into orbit around the sun, while the U.S. was still fumbling toward that puny lob into lower space called Project Mercury. People in Scandinavia were outliving us, and East Germans were faster in the backstroke. And while it's impossible to pinpoint the moment when the postwar era proper ended and the geoeconomic age began, a pretty good case can be made that it happened in 1959.

That year France racked up its first U.S. trade surplus in six decades. Japan became a creditor nation for the first time in its modern history, and the Bank of Tokyo established a beachhead in Los Angeles. The Soviet economy, which Americans, as an article of faith, still thought of as a sluggish giant bereft of all incentives, was growing twice as fast as ours, and while the Dow Jones average was advancing at a respectable annual rate of 15 percent, prices on the Frankfurt exchange were nearly doubling. When, in 1959, a U.S. trade delegation visited the newly independent nation of Nyasaland, expecting to be greeted as the bearers of all things bright and beautiful, they found that committees from not one, not two, but *six* exporting countries had already been there with their sample cases.

The comeuppance was already on the way, though it would come on slowly, simmering hardly noticed through the best of times. There would be nothing of the cataclysm about it, nothing abrupt or even, in theory, unforeseeable. It would, in reality, be only a leveling, but would feel like a beating, a stalemate that would seem like a humiliation. Under its stresses, consensus would inexorably crack and old alliances would crumble. Already by 1959 two thirds of the '49ers were expressing "flat disapproval" of their former hero Ike. They were disappointed with Congress and disgusted with the unions, and in this barely beginning atmosphere of blame the more candid '49ers would open up a window in their implacable self-assurance and wonder aloud if their brand of hard-nosed competence was the best of tools for dealing with the subtler situations ahead. Maybe the wisdom of Ad Prac was not, after all, an adequate wisdom. Maybe the glad passions of the Postwar

Code had been a little shrill. It was getting harder to avoid admitting certain doubts, harder not to murmur certain qualms.

At the bottom of the 1959 Class survey, underneath the neat, short lines of quantitative data, there was a space reserved for personal comments, and one '49er, responding anonymously, wrote as follows: "I find myself . . . doing a barely adequate job as a businessman, a barely adequate job in raising my children and being a husband, a barely adequate job in paying bills, [and making] no creative contribution whatsoever."

PART II

Comeuppance

six

The Old Sausage Game

"You know what they taught us at the Business School?" says Len Caust. "Never in quite as many words, of course. But what they taught us was how to play the old sausage game. You know what the old sausage game is?"

Caust lifts an eyebrow, crosses his knees, waits. He knows how to work an audience. What he'd set out to be as a young man, in fact, was an actor. In World War II he'd been an infantry lieutenant stationed in France. Upon demobilization, the Army, since it couldn't get everybody home at once anyway, allowed people to start using their GI educational benefits right there in Europe if they wanted. Guys applied to the Sorbonne, to Oxford, to the University of Milan. Len Caust, alone of all the American soldiers on the Continent, applied to London's Royal Academy of Dramatic Art. There he did Shakespeare, Ibsen,

Shaw. He worked on vocal technique, on gesture, on improvisation. He was going to be, if not a star, then certainly a journeyman performer in the dignified and unhysterical British mold. He had the day's requisite dark wavy hair and a long open face somewhat suggestive of the young Jimmy Stewart. He could dance.

So he put in his afternoons at RADA, and when he came back to the States, it was to pound the pavements of Broadway and do the occasional soft-shoe or bedroom farce on the straw-hat circuit. In 1947 as today, however, acting was a dicey business. Open auditions called forth hordes of singers, comics, romantic leads, nearly all of whom had at least a modicum of talent. They wore two-toned shoes, they'd gladly spend their lunch money on a boutonniere, and their only fear in life was having to wire home for bus fare back to Dayton. Len Caust might have been one of the few to hit it or one of the many who would ride the Greyhound; he decided not to wait around to find out which would happen first. Doubting his own vocation, he went to the B School by default. It was sort of ironic: while other guys were clamoring to get in, enduring sleepless nights of alternating hope and fear, Caust settled for a Harvard MBA because it was a lot easier than landing a part as a second banana Off Broadway. At Soldiers Field he entertained his classmates with his prowess at juggling and his deftness as a mime.

"So here's what the sausage game is," he resumes. "You win yourself a market with a nice all-meat sausage, the best sausage you can make. People eat that sausage and they say hm-hm. So now you've established the product, right? Now you can afford to start slipping in some

sawdust. Add the sawdust by small enough increments
and no one'll even notice. They'll still say hm-hm, because
people are creatures of habit. Of course, five or six increments down the road you'll end up with a product that
bears little or no resemblance to what you started with, but
you'll get away with it. For a while at least. Your market
share will hold, your margin will increase, and everybody
will think you're smart. I've seen it happen."

Caust retired in 1980 as manager of the Marketing Information Services Department at Lever Brothers. His position, by almost any standard, was one of considerable
eminence. By the stiff criteria of HBS '49, however, he was
one of those upper-middle-management guys who didn't
quite catch fire. For a while he'd been in the thick of it.
Right after B School, in fact, Len Caust had had one of the
Class's hottest jobs, working for Daniel Starch, the virtual
inventor of market research and a pioneer in the statistical
models that would come to play such a pivotal role in the
decision-making processes of U.S. companies. More than
almost anyone, Caust had been in the vanguard of the
modern way of doing business; he'd helped define what
modern was all about.

But at some point Len Caust's prospects seemed to
fade; at some indistinct but crucial juncture he seemed to
have held back from really signing on with the corporate
agenda. Those elegantly abstract numerical formulas—it
was intriguing to think them through and map them out,
but when it came time to conduct business according to
their dictates, Len Caust felt uneasy. By the end, when he
was eased into early retirement by a flab-cutting task force
of which he himself was a member, it was clear that his at-

titudes had become irreconcilably out of step with those of a major U.S. company doing consumer business in the 1970s. Len Caust had become archaic.

"Maybe it's a ridiculous comparison," he says, "but I still think of a lot of things in terms of theater. Theater can't exist without trust, unless the audience—the consumer, that is —really believes that the actors are doing their best, putting on as good a show as they can because they respect the people watching. Well, in business your average 'actor' despises the consumer and doesn't seem to care especially about the quality of the show. Your average MBA sees the consumer as a mark, a factor to be got around. He pays lip service to the notion of providing what the customer wants, because that's what he's *supposed* to talk about—publicly.

"But look, I've spent my life in closed-door meetings with these people, and I'll tell you what really gets their juices flowing: it's these arcane statistical formulas that have nothing whatsoever to do with the customer *or* the product. *New Improved!* How many times have you heard that one? But come on—the real energy doesn't go into improving anything, it goes into figuring out how to make it cheaper and advertise it better. Take this little piece of hardware, make it thinner, make it lighter. It isn't going to work as well, it isn't going to last as long, but oh boy, we're gonna sell a lot of 'em. Is that business? That's bullshit. That's the sausage game. But that's basically what goes on. I'm glad, in a way, that the Japanese have been rubbing our noses in it lately, because at least they've shown that the American consumer isn't quite as stupid as a lot of American businessmen seem to think; that, in the long run, the quality job will still win out."

The quality job, of course, used to be an American specialty. Through the forties and on into the years of the long honeymoon, American products were the world's standard, the nonpareil; anything else was cheap imitation, mimicry that didn't quite come off. Made in U.S.A. meant that it wouldn't shrink in the dryer, that it would write through butter, that it would keep on ticking even when attached to the propeller of an outboard engine. With these assurances came a secure and rosy glow not just of prosperity but of self-esteem—a self-esteem that was reinforced every time a guy with six grand to spend passed up a Jaguar or a BMW in favor of the lumbering splendor of a Chrysler Imperial or an Olds 98 loaded to the gills with options. As late as 1960, imported manufactured goods comprised a minuscule 1.8 percent of total U.S. sales (as opposed to nearly 15 percent in 1985). In machinery, in electronics, in steel, in textiles, American products were *it*. Pharmaceuticals, chemicals, sporting goods, blue jeans—about the only things Americans didn't make best were the things it was beneath their dignity to make at all, things like paper umbrellas for mai tais and fifty-nine-cent rubber sandals for the beach.

Then the situation changed. Exactly when it changed is impossible to say, since a great deal of time and money, as well as heroic exertions of the national ego, went into ignoring the fact. Certainly by the mid-seventies, however, it was unshirkably clear that the shift had come, that the big time was losing air and the comeuppance was already well advanced.

Foreign competition was applying the squeeze, and not just with cheaper goods—that's what Japs and Taiwanese were *for,* after all—but with better ones. Sony was no baloney, while Motorola (before it was taken over by the Japanese company Matsushita) was turning out more defects than televisions—140 goofs per 100 sets. While the American suburbs were abuzz with conversations about the reliability of Datsuns and Toyotas, certain Detroit products were shown to have a melancholy propensity to explode when nudged from behind. The city of New York ended up suing Rockwell International to the tune of $72 million because of a shipment of subway cars that turned out to be turkeys, while Cleveland gave its contract to an Italian firm which underbid the Americans and whose train had the not inconsiderable advantage of staying on the tracks. Even in the much vaunted high-tech industries, American firms were getting aced out; a 1980 study indicated that American computer memory chips were five to six times as likely to fail as their Japanese counterparts; U.S. companies congratulated themselves for tightening up and, by year's end, reducing the ratio to three-to-one.

The stories of American flops piled up like bones in a mass grave, and the damning figures on quality soon began to translate more or less directly into market-share statistics. In 1980, 28 percent of all autos sold in the U.S. were imported, as opposed to 6 percent as recently as 1965. Eighty percent of America's watches were foreign-made, up from 48 percent in 1970. Thirty percent of our athletic equipment came from abroad, as did 90 percent of our CB radios and motorcycles (Dad, what's a Harley-Davidson?) and virtually 100 percent of new consumer electronics such as video cassette recorders. Worse still, public-opinion surveys indicated that the trend away from domestic goods was nowhere near its peak. A 1980 study sponsored by the American Society for Quality Control reported that fully one half of U.S. consumers were discontent with domestic goods, and that over a quarter believed that foreign products were better. Only 39 percent of the respondents gave American appliances high marks for quality; American cars got a thumbs-up from only 17.6 percent.

Embarrassed, baffled, frustrated, and terrified, the various constituencies of American enterprise addressed their mutual problems in the time-honored democratic way: they called each other names. Suddenly everybody was a villain. American management tumbled from its position of peak prestige and began to be portrayed as a pathetic pack of blundering clowns. Unions, addicted to automatic cost-of-living raises but disaddicted to productivity, were stupidly and shortsightedly bleeding industry dry. Congress was a bunch of wimps who regulated things too much and didn't realize that a tax on profits was a tax on progress. The administration, seduced by its own cowboy-capitalist fantasies, couldn't get it through its head that there was no such thing as a free and open market, internationally speaking.

Everyone had a point to make and everyone had a finger to point, so far as the quality lag and its consequences were concerned. But, in the midst of all the squirming and recriminations, the most basic point of all seemed to go overlooked by almost everyone. The quality of American goods slipped—or, to put it more precisely, failed to keep pace with the improvements made elsewhere—for the simple reason that, once the blithe days of the long honeymoon got rolling, quality ceased to be a high priority either of management *or* of labor *or* of government. Once American dominion had been established, the subject was not much thought about, period; in a vastly affluent and largely uncompetitive time, it didn't have to be. The old sausage game was working just fine, and plain American horse sense dictated that you didn't fix something that wasn't broke. If quality had been thought of as a good *unto itself*, things might have been different; but apparently it hadn't been.

The problem, then, was not one of mechanics or even economics exactly, but of values. Exactly the sort of values—subjective, unquantifiable, sticky—that the "modern" approach to business prided itself on ironing out of the decision-making machinery.

"It really isn't that mysterious," says Len Caust, pushing himself forward by the arms of his chair, then gesturing as if slashing chalk onto a blackboard. "Think of it as algebra. Remember when they gave you those long, complicated equations to solve? How did you solve 'em? The trick was to line things up in such a way that most of the factors canceled out—remember? The more factors you could just eliminate, the simpler the problem got. Well, that's how we learned business.

"Certain factors *had* to stay. Costs, analyses of what the competition was up to—you couldn't very well eliminate *them*. But quality? Look, it could be demonstrated—*proved*—tha' you could make a profit at the top of the market or you could make a profit at the bottom of the market. You could, in theory, make money at *any* level of quality—which meant, conveniently enough, that quality could get canceled out of the equation. You see? You might have your personal preferences, but it would be made very clear to you that personal preferences were not what business was about. One thing about business—it isn't snobby. A guy who makes a million bucks in, say, the perfect button-down shirt or the finest surgical instrument is no higher on the ladder than the guy who makes a million bucks selling potato chips without any potatoes in 'em. There's a saying that sums it up, maybe you've heard it: One man's shit is another man's bread and butter."

Not that quality, in at least certain of its aspects, was a consideration necessarily incompatible with the statistically oriented, mass-market philosophy which held sway after the war, and of which the men of '49 were proselytes, beneficiaries, and ultimately victims. Even before Pearl Harbor a former U.S. Census Bureau mathematician named W. Edwards Deming had developed a system whereby the costs and value-added of quality control could be analyzed numerically and factored into the "scientific" way of running a company. Deming's schema had nothing to say about the essential validity of a product; it dealt only with uniformity, reliability, the maintenance of an agreed-upon standard. But even this degree of concern with quality seemed to annoy American managers, whose reaction, according to *Fortune,* was "Go away, Deming, we're making money."

So Deming did go away. Specifically, he went away to Japan, where he was embraced as a prophet. The Deming Prize for quality control, awarded annually since 1950, is considered so important in that country that its bestowal is broadcast on national TV, like the Oscars.

But who knew? The chance offered by Deming was just one more opportunity that the America of the day could well afford to pass up. The era of the throwaway culture was dawning—and to a generation whose childhood Christmases had been Depression-stingy and who then had to keep darning the same stockings and resoling the same sad pair of shoes through the war, that was perfectly fine. People didn't *want* a dress that would last more than one year. They didn't want a car that they wouldn't be ready to trade in after two, because they wanted the thrill of buying a car *again*. Secretly, American housewives hoped that their toasters would go on the fritz, so they could buy a four-slice job next time, the kind that lowered the toast by itself. Planned obsolescence—the phrase has come to represent everything cynical, shabby, stupid, and calamitous about the priorities of American business at midcentury; the fact is, however, that planned obsolescence was just another way of saying give the people what they want. From the perspective of the fifties, it seemed that there would always be plenty of money to rebuy the shorted-out radios and cracked plastic cameras, and no one had begun to ask whether there'd be enough incinerators and landfills to burn or bury all the junk that was used up, worn out, frayed around the buttonholes, or that people had just got sick of looking at. The distance between the checkout counter and the garbage can was getting ever shorter; the only implication of that fact seemed to be that people would go shopping again that much sooner.

And, for a quarter-century or so, they did. Then three things happened, more or less at once. Real disposable income stopped growing. Foreign goods and foreign marketing reached a level of sophistication that made them truly competitive with the homegrown. And the American consumer, like the kid who finally realizes that steak is better food than candy, was growing up. Gradually, the claim that a Volvo would last twelve years came to seem more important than that next year's Pontiac would have a different configuration of taillights. The Panasonic stereo that sounded good was preferable to the Zenith that looked like a continuation of the breakfront. American consumer business, it was becoming clear, had made a major wrong turn at the intersection of quality and flash, and it was starting to pay for the error in spades. The irony was that the businessmen who'd set the throwaway tone of the long honeymoon had just been doing what they'd been taught, often at the expense of their own tastes. *They* preferred a good cotton oxford to polyester, an honest fountain pen to a cheapo ballpoint that leaked ink in your pocket. But in keeping with the tenets of modern scientific management, they'd steered clear of such subjective, sentimental judgments and followed the so-called wisdom of the marketplace. It apparently could not be factored into the equation that the marketplace itself might wise up as time went on.

By 1980 or so, in light of such realizations, it had come to be open season on American management. Economists and sociologists pointed out disturbing correspondences between America's quality skid and the rise of its professional managerial class. *The New York Times Magazine* did a cover story in 1981 chronicling the fall from world prestige of the American executive. Meanwhile, it had become all the rage to study Japanese management, on the premise that if *we* were wrong, they *must* be right. Even the business-education establishment itself was slipping into the hair shirt. H. Edward Wrapp, lately of the faculty at HBS, went on record in *Dun's Review* as saying "we have created a monster. . . . The business schools have done more to insure the success of the Japanese and West German invasion of America than any one thing I can think of."* They'd done it, in Wrapp's view, by "producing a horde of managers with . . . talents that are not in the mainstream of the enterprise . . . [and] the tragedy is that these talents mask real deficiencies in overall management capabilities. These talented performers run for cover when grubby operating decisions must be made and often fail miserably."†

Somewhere along the line, in the increasing abstraction of business priorities from production to marketing to running the numbers, some vital animating spark had been lost. Purpose had given place to mere technique, a glozing efficiency was standing in for real effectiveness— and the men of '49, in this as in so many things, found themselves at the fulcrum of the seesaw, arrayed in their various attitudes along the cusp of the change. Some '49ers, as part of the general unquestioning leap into what had passed for modernity, could not but see themselves as part of the problem. Others, who had remained steadfast in the ethos of the widget and the conveyor, groped for solace in the thought that they'd probably been right all along. Still, it was hard to remain unscathed by the general atmosphere of blame. In 1980 the men of '49 were at a median age of fifty-seven and in most cases were at the very height of their professional powers. Their whole careers, they'd been stroked by the press, loved by their shareholders, voted bonuses by their boards, and vindi-

---

* Don't Blame the System, Blame the Managers," *Dun's Review,* September 1980, p. 88.
  † Ibid., p. 82.

cated by the angles on the graph. Now, rather suddenly, their Alma Mater, many of their most cherished axioms, and in fact their whole generation of business leadership were under attack. And the attacks were potentially lethal.

"For better or worse," says Conrad Jones, whom the years seem only to have confirmed in his relentless objectivity and drop-dead bluntness as to the heart of the matter, "I don't think most of us really let the criticisms sink in. If we *had* . . . ? Well, Jesus, think about the implications of what's being said. Here we are, old guys who've been in charge of things for a while, and for whom it's too late really to undo the things we've done, even if we wanted to. We've been rolling along, feeling pretty good—and now someone is telling us not just that we've hit a snag, but that we'd been screwing up *all along,* and it just took a while for it to show. I mean, that's a serious charge.

"Is it a *fair* charge?" he continues, ticking off the pros and cons as neatly as if they were jotted down before him in two columns on a yellow pad. "It's dodgeable. I mean, partly it's just a media bandwagon thing to dump on American management. Or you can answer the charge with other charges that are, I think, equally persuasive—labor costs, tax structures, pressures that come from Wall Street, and so forth.

"Still, if the basic complaint is that American managers have gotten too caught up in managing *per se,* and not caught up enough in their products and their customers, then I don't see how I can deny that my generation of guys from the B School have been part of the problem. I mean, for the real dyed-in-the-wool professional manager, there's nothing illogical about getting a promotion from number-three guy at ABC company that makes macaroni to number-two guy at XYZ company that makes fan belts. I know guys who are proud of the fact that they've never been inside the plants of companies they run. And stuff like that is part of the problem."

Connie Jones has worked with more than five hundred businesses in his three and a half decades of consulting. He's worked with companies on the way up and companies on the way down, companies whose problems he could solve and companies whose problems he saw as terminal. ("What *else* do you enjoy doing?" is the way he begins debriefings with the chiefs of those outfits.) He's worked with companies in sunset industries and in sunrise industries, companies that were acquiring and companies that were divesting. In his view, however, none of those distinctions is what really defines the feel and style of a business, what the business is really *about;* the single most crucial point in understanding what makes a company tick is whether that company is family-run or professionally managed.

"You know," he says, "when we were in school, it was still pretty much the norm that companies were run by families, and it was more or less the exception that they were run by outside experts. The shift was already on, and had been, I guess, since the twenties. But the archetype of the American company still had the classic elements: the tinkerer who comes up with a smart idea, puts it together in his garage, stamps the family name all over it, and then ends up as the rich and cranky old patriarch whose portrait hangs over the desk that his son, his grandson, and his great-grandson will eventually sit at. That's the traditional American business. That's what *made* American business. And what's been going on for as long as I've been out in the field is that we just keep getting farther and farther away from that.

"But here's the thing," he goes on, raising an explanatory finger. "Today, with a lot of industries in trouble, we're nostalgic—and rightly so—for those kinds of old-fashioned, rock-solid businesses. But no one was nostalgic about them thirty years ago. They were old-fashioned, period. Nothing was easier than pointing out their obvious deficiencies. They were blundering little Mom-and-Pop operations where half the time the inheriting son was a flake and the daughter broke the family's heart by marrying beneath herself. They didn't do research, they didn't keep up. They paid more taxes than they had to because they were in the Dark Ages of accounting. True, they may have made the best damn products on the market, but still . . .

"The point I'm getting at is that there's a whole different value system that pertains. The family-run companies—companies like Maytag, Cessna Aircraft, Johnson's Wax—are driven by a value system that's an extension of *family* values. The point being that after you make sure that everybody in the family has a roof over their head and enough money to fall back on, what's still important? What's important is reputation, your good name in the community, nationally, even internationally. And what's reputation based on but quality over time? The professionally managed companies don't have anywhere near the same commitment to quality, because they don't have anywhere near the same sense of duration. What's the average executive tenure these days—five years? You can get away with a pretty lousy product if all you're aiming at is five years.

"Here, let me tell you about two meetings I sat in on. Both were with companies that were having some problems with quality control. One company was professionally managed. Their approach to the problem was to analyze everything. How many doors, say, were falling off? What *percentage* of doors were falling off? How much would it cost to stick 'em back on? What were the chances of getting sued? How much advertising would it take to counteract the bad publicity? Not once did they actually talk about the doors, the hinges, or why the hell they were falling off. They weren't interested in solving the problem, they just wanted to manage the mess.

"The other meeting was at Coleman Stove," Jones continues, "which is family-run. They were having a problem with some boilers that were cracking. So picture it— the executive committee assembles, there's the usual small talk, how're the kids, how's the golf game. Then the service department comes in with the reports, the clipboards, the yellow pencils, and everybody hunkers down for a serious discussion. Well, you know how long that meeting lasted? About thirty seconds. Old Man Coleman sits bolt upright in his chair and bellows out, 'You mean we got goods out there that aren't working? Get 'em back, replace 'em, and find out why, goddammit.' And that was the end of the meeting. There was no financial analysis. There was no legal analysis. There was no customer-relations analysis. There was *no* goddam analysis. The issue was the integrity of the product—which meant there was no issue at all. You stand by it, and that's that."

The integrity of the product—an appealing concept, but one that can hardly be thought of as central in an age of nondairy whipped topping and furniture made of wood-grain plastic veneers glued onto slabs of particle board. Not that quality goods have gone out of existence; it's just that they've been pushed farther and farther to the fringe, have become the quaint exception. Quality has become a cult, and, like all cults, it defines itself by its variance from the norm. A taste for well-made things has become ever more synonymous with a taste for antiques. When Connie Jones is in New York, he lives in an old building overlooking the East River, a building with the thick walls, parquet floors, and notched moldings that Manhattan apartments stopped having along about the 1950s. The windows are the sort of small-paned leaded glass that no one bothers to make anymore; there is a custom-fitted window seat that no contemporary builder would bother to install. In the living room there is a fireplace with the distinguishing rarity of a real oak mantel, and in the fireplace Jones burns wood he carries down from Connecticut rather than the ersatz "logs" offered for sale in urban supermarkets.

"Look," says Connie Jones, "when most of us got to the Business School, we had no idea *what* we wanted to manage; all we knew was *that* we wanted to manage. And that seemed fine, because the way it was presented to us was that managing was a skill unto itself. Like driving rivets. If you could drive rivets, you could drive 'em into pairs of blue jeans or into the Verrazano Bridge. The exact application didn't really matter. Logistically, I guess that's the way management *had* to be taught. I mean, there were so many different things we might conceivably end up doing, the School really had no choice but to take the stand that the things we were learning could be applied to *any* of them. Management itself was the keystone. If you managed well, other things would take care of themselves.

"That was the premise we started with," says Connie Jones, stirring up the fire with a brass poker, "and we worked from it diligently and in some cases brilliantly. We took that premise about as far as it could possibly be taken.

"Only problem was, the premise turned out to be wrong."

seven

So Who Is
Kidding Who Here?

There were other premises as well in the '49er canon.

One of them was the notion that, of all the paths a businessman might take, none was as high, bold, and worthy of respect as that of innovator, risk taker, initiator of an enterprise. That was the finest thing a man could do, the ambition that jibed most closely with the postwar vision of endless progress and expansion, and more than six '49ers out of ten had named it as their goal while at Soldiers Field. The School, in turn, was behind them all the way. It offered a second-year elective called Management of New Enterprises. It made all the proper obeisances to the entrepreneur as hero, the guy whose guts and imagination fired the furnace, and who had the best chance of ending up with his bust in bronze in the lobbies of large buildings that would bear his name.

"But when push came to shove," says Ned Dewey, one of the relative handful of '49ers who actually did end up being their own bosses, "most of us either didn't have the nerve to go it alone or couldn't come up with an idea that seemed worth chasing. And those of us who did found out that the School hadn't prepared us at all for the day-to-day mucking around with a start-up business. We liked to think of ourselves as adventurers, but come on—we were a bunch of twenty-five-year-olds out of the Army, full of bluster but mainly just wanting a paycheck. And Harvard liked to think of itself as where the action was, a breeding ground for people who'd really make a difference, but come on again—in fact it was a finishing school for GM. So who is kidding who here?"

The answer seems to be that everybody was kidding everybody, up to and including themselves. The '49ers, for all their high spirits and all their jaunty business metaphors drawn from the sports arena, the battlefield, and the poker table, hadn't *really* gone to HBS to turn their futures into a glorious gamble. And HBS wouldn't really have known what to do with them if they had. The truth of the matter was that, then as now, there was a strong, if implicit, anti-risk bias both in institutions like the Harvard Business School and in the great majority of people who were drawn there. The whole thrust of modern management, after all, as John Kenneth Galbraith would observe in *The Affluent Society,* could "be understood only as a comprehensive effort to reduce risk." The adventure, such as it was, lay in trying to find the sure thing; professionalism, by definition, meant that you didn't take more chances than you absolutely had to.

The doctrine was not exactly swashbuckling, nor did it

apparently have to be force-fed to the returning veterans.
There were, in fact, instances when professors berated
students for playing it too close to the vest. Clark Randall,
who went on to become a corporate vice-president with
Hallmark Cards in Kansas City, still remembers a dressing
down his section received at the hands of the wry and occasionally bellicose Georges Doriot. "He'd asked us," Randall recalls, "to list the ten companies we thought had the
most outstanding futures ahead of them. Then he tabulated the results and read them out. Number one was General Motors. Number two was General Electric. Number
three, I think, was U.S. Steel. Doriot read through the list,
then turned on us with that disdainful French curl in his
lower lip. 'You deesgust me,' he said. 'Most of you don't
even desehrve to be in my clahss. Yueh'rhe not wuehrth
my time. Yueh'rhe shortsighted. Yueh'rhe status-con-
scious. Yueh'rhe *borrrhing.* You know somesing? I gave
zat same question to a clahss fifteen yeahrs ago, and you
know what the answers wehre? Number one was Zhen-
eral Motors. . . .' "

But if the '49ers were sometimes overly inclined to try
to please by giving out the orthodox answers, it's equally
true that the Harvard Graduate School of Business Administration, by its very history, was geared toward asking
the orthodox questions.

For all its more recent cachet, it is well to remember
that when HBS limped onto the pedagogical landscape in
1908, it had only the puniest of endowments, and neither
a campus of its own nor a proven constituency in the actual world of commerce. The school's founding philosophy
had consisted of a hunch: that by conferring the dignity of
a Master's degree on the subject of business administra-

tion, "one of the oldest of the arts," to quote former University President A. Lawrence Lowell, could be redefined as "the youngest of the professions."

No matter how prettily it was phrased, however, the concept of bringing business into the scholastic fold faced two not inconsiderable obstacles: businessmen hated academics' guts, and vice versa. To scholars, handing out honorific titles denoting expertise in such squalid processes as psyching out markets, selling widgets, and accumulating wealth was nothing short of abject whoredom. To the day's rugged-individualist businessmen, the thought that any cloistered, wispy-bearded, and probably reform-minded professor could tell them how to run their show was laughable if not grotesque.

That these warring parties could be made to look each other in the eye, let alone to acknowledge that they might in fact be able to learn from one another, is a testament to the persuasiveness of the Business School's creators, who seem to have been past masters of compromise and accommodation. Even case method itself evolved, to a large extent, as part of the pitch for coaxing businessmen and professors to hop into bed together. By studying cases, the practical-minded real-world types could feel that attention was being properly focused on the nitty-gritty, rather than frittered away on texts and theory; and academics, far from being abashed that they were teaching in a field that *had* no texts or theory, could tell themselves that they were helping to build a new intellectual edifice by the time-honored means of deductive reasoning. Something for everybody.

As with every fledgling enterprise, however, the B School's most pressing need in its formative years was customers for its product. The School could not long survive unless the degree it granted was shown to have some tender value in the world at large; and the most likely place for that value to emerge was in the big corporations which, in the years around World War I, were just coalescing into their modern form. To win the corporations over as enthusiastic employers of its graduates, the School had to offer a graduate appropriate to the corporations' specific needs: *not* a wild and crazy visionary, but a cool-headed professional whose job would be to expedite rather than initiate, who would abet, rather than challenge, the smooth, habituated running of ever more complicated organizations, and who, by temperament and skills, would operate at a safe remove from the turf and the ego of the old-fashioned seat-of-the-pants entrepreneur who, chances are, was still the boss. In the original conception, then, the MBA would play Friday to the industry captain's Crusoe. What happened, however, was that the Crusoes died out and, according to a 1983 article in the journal *Business and Society Review,* "were gradually replaced by the products of graduate business schools—a more pusillanimous breed, well trained in the fine art of business mechanics and financial statements but devoid of the jugular instincts of their predecessors."

Pusillanimous, as applied to the Class of '49, is overstating the case. There's no denying, however, that for all the brave dormitory rhetoric about crapshoots and betting the limit and swinging from the heels, the Class showed a strong tendency to end up with safe jobs in big companies in industries that were already mature. For every guy who, like Tom Murphy, took a flyer on a new entry in a field that hadn't yet proved out, there were a dozen who nestled in the bosom of outfits like Procter and Gamble, Sears, Roebuck, or the Morgan Bank. For every wayward soul like Pete McColough, who anted up five years of his life for a front-row seat on a new technology, there were ten who opted for secure slots amid the reassuring solidity of machine tools, lumber, or steel. As of 1959, fully one fourth of the Class was toiling for companies that had ten thousand or more employees. Only seventy-eight men described themselves as self-employed, and the majority of those had either gone into preexisting family operations or simply hung out shingles as accountants or as brokers in insurance or real estate; not more than five had launched enterprises that could really be described as start-up companies. The typical '49er, untrue to his daydreams, had imbedded himself in the belly of an organization whose destiny was separate from and larger than his own.

Moreover, for all the lip service paid to the entrepreneur's crucial contributions, the dollars-and-cents evidence of pay stubs and tax returns was indicating that in fact the guys who'd gone to the big outfits had made the smarter moves; somebody was kidding somebody about how the world of business *really* allocated its rewards. By 1969 the median income of '49ers working for companies that employed twenty thousand souls or more was nearly half again as much as that of guys working for outfits with fifty employees or less—and that included '49ers who owned those companies. By 1974, it's true, owners of firms were disproportionately represented among the Class's roster of millionaires; still, that group constituted only a dozen two-comma types out of nearly a hundred. As a bloc, the best-off guys by far were those who'd climbed the ziggurats of the biggest corporations, and who were pulling down average incomes a third higher than the Class mean. It wasn't mere pusillanimity, then, that transformed the would-be firebrands of 1947 into the organization men of their subsequent careers; it was logic. In the halcyon days of the big time, the simple fact was that the organization had the sweetest favors to bestow. Because of the executive shortage occasioned by the Depression and the war, the route to the top, or damn close to it, was clear; the big corporations back then weren't offering a choice between security and a shot at the big score—they were offering both. And what kind of guy flirts with Chapter 11 as an entrepreneur when the same, or greater, rewards are being offered along with a medical plan, four weeks paid vacation, and the use of a company car? Not the kind that goes to B School in the first place.

Unfortunately, however, the golden age of organizational opportunity was, by its very nature, self-limiting in time. Previously unpeopled paths to corporate power became inevitably glutted. New slots failed to keep pace with the supply of executive talent, because potential founders of companies had settled into serene careers as other people's veeps instead. As of the early seventies—by which time, of course, the men of '49 were above the fray—the corporate logjam had reached stultifying proportions. Even Harvard MBAs, in those years, often found themselves bottlenecked within spitting distance of entry level, and a new wave of entrepreneurial enthusiasm belatedly got cooking—not in response to hyped-up business myths this time, but because of dire necessity.

The myth of the B School entrepreneur also calls into

question two of twentieth-century America's most cherished and least examined clichés: that everything has been changing incredibly fast, and that the American economy is incredibly "dynamic" (whatever that means exactly). In actual fact, what's been incredible about the broad outline of American business, at least through the middle decades of the century, has been its stability and its stasis. Half of the fifty largest U.S. manufacturing firms in 1972 had already been among the fifty largest in 1947; only five hadn't been among the top two hundred. And for an indication of how "dynamic" the economy had actually been, consider that the big companies in every one of these industries—petroleum, rubber, machinery, food products, and transportation equipment—held the *exact same number* of top-two-hundred slots in 1970 as they had in 1920! For all the talk about new directions and new technologies, you could have gone to sleep for half a century and woken up to a business landscape that was quite perfectly familiar. Where were the phenomenal start-up enterprises that might have displaced the giants? It took Silicon Valley to remind us that a meaningful displacement was even possible—and Silicon Valley had been staked out not by natty, polished MBAs, but by abysmally dressed computer nerds who put down roots because they liked the weather in Cupertino and the beaches over at Santa Cruz.

"How can you put a price tag," says Ned Dewey, "on all the companies that never got launched because some MBA decided, 'Ah, fuck it, who needs the aggravation? I'll go work for Du Pont instead'? How can you estimate the jobs that didn't get created, the patents that didn't get followed up on? How can you even *imagine* where we might be today if fewer guys had taken the path of least resistance?"

Not that, in Dewey's view, the only start-up enterprises that matter are the ones that revolutionize whole industries and go down in business history. That, in fact, is precisely his complaint about the Business School's approach to so-called small business. "If you're the kind of small business that grows up into a *huge* business—if you start off fiddling with spare typewriter parts and grow up to be Wang—then they're fascinated, then you make it into the casebook. But there's a Catch-22 here: as long as you're stuck diddling with the difficulties *specific* to small businesses, then they either aren't interested or just don't have any idea what to tell you."

Dewey's particular passion is for the human-scaled operation that keeps alive the tradition of individual opportunity and affords room for the quirks and eccentricities of the individual proprietor. He's served on the national board of the Small Business Administration, and has worked at street level helping out start-up outfits in Boston's black ghetto, Roxbury. As for his own entrepreneurial career, after his apprenticeship with Gulf he went into business first as an oil wholesaler, then as owner of a chain of gas-station-and-convenience-stores in upstate New York, "selling wiper blades and Post Toasties." The stores throw off enough cash so that Dewey can also "have some fun in venture capital," investing in schemes that range from a new company making kits that will allow doctors "to rip off their clients for certain kinds of tests instead of having separate labs rip them off," to a buy-out of "the guy who makes the best pretzels in East Boston." He also owns a piece of an offshore insurance company in Bermuda and says that the tax laws have "forced" him to sink some dollars into gas and oil drilling.

"Look," he says, "I understand why these hotshots who've been raised on fancy math and nine-digit figures don't want to be gritty little entrepreneurs. Let's face it— most of running your own business comes down to questions like 'Do I buy toilet paper by the case and have my employees steal it from me, or do I buy it by the roll and pay a penny more a slice?' It doesn't set the imagination on fire. But on the other hand, if you don't learn how to run something small, how are you supposed to run something big? The fact is we have a lot of people out there who don't know how to run *anything*. They know how to ride shotgun over a *piece* of something. But believe me, that isn't the same thing. Not even close."

Running something big was precisely what Harry Figgie, Jr., of Lakewood, Ohio, decided, at age sixteen, to do with his life. His father had started poor and ended up as a vice-president of Rockwell International. The son was proud of that achievement and held an affectionate awe for the nation and the economic system in which such leaps of fortune could occur. But Figgie Junior was determined to take the upward movement much, much farther. His ambition was tripartite. Starting with zilch, he'd build a major company, something in, say, the billion-dollar range. That accomplished, he'd step back a bit, become president of a university, then at some point Secretary of Commerce.

Toward these sundry goals, he began his academic career with an engineering degree at Cleveland's Case Institute. After a stint in the Army, he had a flirtation with a career as a major-league pitcher—he was drafted by both the Cleveland Indians and the old St. Louis Browns—but decided to pass up the Bigs for the Business School. In 1949 he went to work on the shop floor of a screw company in Chicago, and in the evenings he earned himself, simultaneously, a law degree and a Master's in Industrial Engineering. Then, just to round himself out, he signed on with the Cleveland office of Booz, Allen, where he was told that operations guys virtually never cut it as consultants. Figgie shortly became one of the youngest partners in the history of the firm.

Which brings us up to 1963. In that year a bow-wow of a company called Automatic Sprinkler, which had lost money five years running, came up for sale for $7.2 million. Figgie, for reasons no one else could understand and which even he could never quite explain, decided that the floundering concern would make a perfect cornerstone for his empire. He scraped together $27,000 of his own money, somehow managed to finance the rest, and took the reins. "You're the dumbest man alive," the outgoing board chairman told him. "No, the second," said Figgie. "You sold."

In its first full year under new management, Automatic showed a pretax profit of 9.6 percent on a gross of $25 million, and by 1984 Harry Figgie was presiding over an international conglomerate, pieced together in his image, which consisted of more than forty different operating units, employed 12,500 people, and had annual sales of almost $700 million. Alone among the men of '49, Figgie had gone the way of the old-style blood-and-guts industrial pharaoh. And, more than any of his classmates' stories, Figgie's is one of intensely personal success—sort of.

The Automatic turnaround had attracted a considerable amount of notice, and in 1966 Figgie cashed in on the publicity by taking his company public under the name A-T-O, Incorporated. In those go-go days an awful lot of money could be raised on the strength of a one-shot reputation, and A-T-O soon found itself flush enough to set out on an acquisitions spree like something out of "Let's Make a Deal" on Benzedrine. As an acquisitor, Harry Figgie was a paradox. No one could doubt his erudition or the breadth of his knowledge, yet he seemed to go purely on instinct, even on whim. He bought what he liked, and a lot of it seemed like toys. He loved baseball so much that he bought out Rawlings for mitts and Adirondack for bats. He'd always had a thing for fire engines, so he added to his stable American LaFrance; on the day that A-T-O got listed on the Big Board, he showed up in front of the New York Stock Exchange riding a hook-and-ladder and wearing a helmet. He liked tennis enough to pick up Fred Perry and was enough of a golfer to covet Toney Penna clubs. But mostly Harry Figgie loved industry, smokestack industry, the heavier the better, and he soon started going after road graders, mining tractors, foundries, cement mixers, gears and sprockets, cranes. In all, he scarfed up seventy-two companies in five years, as well as shelling out for five new start-ups.

The sheer aggressiveness of the A-T-O approach rattled some of the more conservative analysts of business strategies, who were critical of Figgie's buying binge. Figgie answered them with characteristic directness. "Hypocrites!" he said. "If you're an old company that sees the need of going into different product lines, they call you *diversified* and say you're smart. If you're a *new* company that's *based* on different product lines, they call you a *conglomerate*, as if it were a dirty word. The hell with 'em."

Not that all or even most of Wall Street objected to the Figgie philosophy. It was hard to argue with results, and the A-T-O chemistry, however odd, seemed to work just fine. By 1968 the company's price/earnings ratio was a glamorous fifty; its stock—founders' shares, of which Figgie himself owned roughly 325,000, had cost eight cents—was selling at a high of seventy-four; and Figgie himself, in the parlance of the day, was being hailed as a "supersynergist."

Then the bottom fell out. Harry Figgie had jauntily projected a per-share earning of $2.75 for 1969; he delivered one of nine pennies. The disparity was tough to explain away, and it ended the A-T-O honeymoon as effectively as a dose of STD. By early 1970 the stock had nosedived to six, and the company name stank to high heaven. A-T-O, in Wall Street's revised appraisal, was just one more bloated, blurry, slapped-together outfit that didn't know what it was about, and Harry Figgie began to be portrayed as just one more kamikaze acquirer who only looked smart as long as he was irrigated with fresh infusions of other people's money.

The fiscal debacle was only part of the company's headaches at that juncture. Alongside it, scandals were brewing and a corporate Figgiegate was threatening to unfold. A-T-O was under scrutiny from the SEC for having taken into account, in its 1967 earnings statement, a company it didn't acquire until 1968. It came out in the wash that A-T-O had been technically bankrupt twice, and once Figgie didn't even know it, reportedly because of some records that were lost. Worst of all, it could be documented that the crash in the stock price had been preceded by a wave of insider selling that stayed just within the letter of the law. By January of 1968 Figgie himself had unloaded eighty thousand shares. The brokerage house that had underwritten A-T-O's original stock offering had sold off a quarter-million. A-T-O's first bank—the Cosmos Bank, of Zurich—had profited a tidy $20 million by its timely liquidations. By 1973 both the stock house and the bank, their reputations reeking, were out of business. No charges were brought; still, it was not a pretty picture, and Harry Figgie decided that a radical lowering of his profile was in order. No more wisecracks to the press; no more rides on fire trucks; no more supersynergistical schemes sung out with panache. For much of the seventies Harry Figgie seemed simply to have vanished.

It was his abiding love for the national pastime that eventually flushed him out. In 1978 the Boston Red Sox came up for sale, and Harry Figgie suddenly made the news again with a bid—unsuccessful, as it turned out—of $18.7 million. If you knew Figgie, you knew his mouth was watering at the thought of owning a major-league franchise, period; but you couldn't very well say that to Wall Street. So Figgie tried to justify the intended acquisition by talking about its public-relations value; "We would have been known all over the country," he said at the time. But Figgie had made a lot of smart people look dumb in the past, and now those people were skeptical of his recipes. "Known for what?" snuffled *Forbes*. "For being a conglomerate that included a baseball team?"

Still, it was clear that the Figgie who reemerged at the
end of the seventies was a man who'd cooled his jets and
put his house in order. He hadn't made a major buy in
nearly a decade. He'd brought A-T-O's debt situation back
from the brink of the debilitating. He'd organized the company's various divisions into a structure that made it seem
less of a free-for-all. He could, in 1978—even with his
stock price still mired at fourteen—announce to the world
that A-T-O was "in danger of becoming a good company."
Forbes parried the claim with the suggestion that the
process of convincing anyone of that might have less to do
with Figgie's substantive efforts than with "Wall
Street['s] . . . short memory." In order, perhaps, to assist
that memory in forgetting, in 1981 Harry Figgie cast false
modesty aside and allowed A-T-O to be rechristened Figgie
International.

By that year, common shares were scrabbling back up
toward the twenty-dollar mark, and income was a respectable $25+ million on the company's high-water annual
sales of roughly $770 million. The press, fickle but not un-
forgiving, especially at times when good news is in short
supply, started making nice again. "Thriving Conglomerate" ran the headline in *Barron's* over a piece that, while it
stopped short of reviving the synergy baloney, lavished
praise on Figgie's savvy as a diversifier. *Nation's Business*
was even more panegyrical, portraying him as a tireless visionary building "his dream company." The *Wall Street
Journal* saw fit, under the heading "Figgie's Opinions," to
provide a forum for the chairman's hellfire-and-brimstone
sermons as to the perils of the federal deficit and the ine-
quities of international trade.

So Figgie was back, out there again as a brash

proselytizer for the prerogatives of business, as a blustery pragmatist full of down-home homilies, as a bit of a hero, a bit of a buffoon, a bit of a gadfly and a bit of a prophet. He said what he thought, he didn't care who minded. He'd make some deathly pessimistic statement, follow it up with a big, carnivorous, Teddy Roosevelt sort of smile, and leave it to the listener to decide if he was serious or not. With his raucous energy, his clear-framed glasses, and his flourishing head of swept-back hair, Figgie made it easy to forget that he was scudding past the age of sixty, and that he was, when you thought about it, of a slightly older generation than were most of the entrepreneurial hotshots around him. It made him different. The younger men tended to be financial guys who'd come of age when it was already accepted wisdom that juggling assets was really the key to making a conglomerate go. Figgie was an operations guy; he could crunch the numbers when he had to, but it wasn't where his heart was. He'd pieced together his empire lathe by lathe and smelter by smelter, realizing but not seeming to care very much that the future was being scaled down to micro and mini. He stayed with the stuff he liked. If you could apply the word "quaint" to something almost a billion dollars big, then there was something quaint about Figgie International, and something poignant about the swaggering dinosaur who ran it. Figgie remained defiantly loyal to things that were curling in around the edges. He was a man who bucked his own prophecies.

There was no one more American than Harry Figgie, Jr. He used to have Norman Rockwell illustrate his annual reports. He put up a goalpost in his backyard so his kids could practice placekicks. His idea of a perfect vacation was a few days exploring Williamsburg, and his corporate headquarters was carefully modeled on Colonial originals. When Figgie talked industry, he was talking *American* industry, the clanking, rattling, steamrolling industry of midcentury. He was talking foundries, conveyors, specialty steel—exactly those businesses that were getting most severely hammered as the long-deferred comeuppance was socking in. Between 1981 and 1982 Figgie's sales were sliced by more than $60 million; nearly three thousand employees got the ax. Consumer business, industrial sales, exports—everything was down. In 1983 again, assets, earnings, personnel were all reduced. It would almost have been better had something really disastrous happened, something you could devise a brave new strategy for dealing with. But this didn't qualify as a disaster, only a subtle but inexorable diminution. Things were proceeding more or less as usual, except that almost everything was shrinking.

And in America, things were only supposed to grow. That had been a central tenet of the postwar faith, and Harry Figgie had clung to that belief perhaps more ferociously than any other member of the Class of '49. Other '49ers, confronted by the diceyness and the exposure of really getting out there and going it alone, had shied away at the last. It was, finally, beneath their dignity or beyond their nerve to get down and wrestle in the mud, to use their mastery of Ad Prac not for petty gambits in the office but for serious battle in the grand arena of the world. Only Harry Figgie, cranky, abrasive, stubborn as a Renaissance Pope, had plied that high road toward the dream—and now it seemed to be the dream itself that was backing down, retreating from its promise.

"We're getting clobbered," Harry Figgie says of America's competitive position in those industries that once had been its virtually sole domain. "What we're engaged in is a global economic war. And we're losing it. Steel's a disaster. Forging's a disaster. Our machine-tool business has been totally destroyed.

"Why? Because we're stand-alone guys and we're not getting help from our government. Yeah, that's right— this is an old *laissez-faire* conservative talking. But conditions change. And what I say now is what's the difference between underwriting a guy on welfare and underwriting a *job* by supporting some form of protectionism? We've got to understand that we're not competing against foreign companies; we're competing against foreign *countries*. Do you know that I can't get a baseball glove into Japan? I can't get a baseball *bat* into Japan. I can't get a friggin' *baseball* into Japan. We have this thing about free trade— hell, I used to believe it, too. Well, there's no such thing. And we better wake up to that."

The consequences of not waking up to it, in Figgie's view, would extend far beyond the relative decline of American manufacturing. Political stability, he believes, would go the way of economic clout. "I could write you a scenario," he says, "in which all of Latin America would go Communist in the next five to ten years. I could write you a scenario for the demise of England in the 1990s when their oil runs out—and how would we look in Europe if we stood by powerless while our best ally went down the tubes? I could write you a scenario in which—if they don't get the deficit and the trade balance in order— there could actually be a different form of government *in this country* by the year 2000."

Yet Figgie, despite his occasional forays into apocalyptic augury, doesn't live like a man braced against the end of time. He runs his company, he follows the pennant races, and he generally keeps his toothy smile in place through the direst of his predictions. Though Figgie will acknowledge that even his own ambitions have had to be scaled down through the years because of the grinding weight of cumulative circumstance. "Around five years out of Business School," he says, "I realized that I probably wouldn't get around to being a college president. Five years more and I'd scratched Secretary of Commerce, too—I'd been to Washington and I wanted no part of that squirrel cage; they'd have eaten me alive.

"So I guess I never got farther than ambition number one. What I turned out to be is what I *started* out to be: a businessman. Well, so be it. Look, my bag is industry, and if it comes to that, I'm content to go down carrying that flag."

eight

Wallpaper Days, or
The Strategy of Decadence

Ernie Henderson III was discharged from the Navy at three o'clock one afternoon in 1946, and at seven p.m. he went to work as a busboy at one of his father's hotels. As far as the younger Henderson was concerned, dinner hour of that evening was the beginning of his life. Other guys fresh out of the service might have felt restless and confused, but Henderson was singleminded as a salmon. He knew exactly what he wanted from his destiny: his father's job. And he knew that he would get that job in due time. He was the son and heir, and though for now he might be scraping plates and weaving under trays the size of kettledrums, this was no B-movie pretense of starting at the bottom. He was being groomed to rule, and that was that.

Besides, he *liked* being a busboy. He liked the Chaplinesque transitions between the decorum of the dining room and the chaos of the kitchen, with broilers occasionally catching fire and lewd remarks sizzling back and forth between the waitresses and the cooks. He liked the institutional-sized grills and fry pans, as handsome in their epic scale as the reels that are used in catching marlin. He liked those things as much as he liked the mountains of crisp starched linen down in Housekeeping, or the ceiling-high stacks of gilt-framed chairs that were kept on dollies in storage closets off the ballroom, or the conspiratorial feel of the little office behind the front desk, where the clerks retreated to smoke and do imitations of the customers. Ernie Henderson, who had grown up playing hide-and-seek in lobbies and doing somersaults over acres of fresh towels, delighted in all those things, and not just because they represented his family's fortune. Hotels were things of life and breath to him; he loved them to the marrow of his bones.

Business School was exile, as far as Henderson was concerned. Some of the Class's other heirs seemed to regard the two-year stint at Harvard as their last whiff of freedom before entering the golden cage of the family firm. Some would try to fend off the inevitable by going through the charade of a few years' seasoning at someone *else's* family firm. Not Henderson. He couldn't wait to go straight back to Sheraton Hotels. By 1958 he'd been appointed treasurer. In 1963 he was named president, one step removed from the throne his father still occupied as CEO and chairman. Henderson Senior, however, showed no signs of readiness to step down. The old man was gentle, he was benign, he was utterly immovable. And he stayed planted in the chairman's office until he quietly keeled over in 1967, at which point his son assumed control.

Within months Ernie Henderson would have given up control of Sheraton. In hardly more than a year he'd be through with the company altogether. Sheraton Hotels would be part of ITT.

"My father's body wasn't even cold," Ernie Henderson recalls, "when they first came sniffing around. ITT's ambitions were pretty grand back then. They wanted to own a leading company in every industry. Sheraton was supposed to provide the hospitality. We were supposed to keep our smiles frozen in place and deal with the public as if things were like they'd always been."

That it was ITT that first approached Henderson had at least partly to do with the fact that the Henderson family's Cape Cod summer place abutted that of Harold Geneen, ITT's founder and chairman. It was a prestigious address, to be sure, but it was also a little like living next door to the Blob. Geneen had a way of engulfing anything he came into contact with. He'd put out a pseudopod, open up a membrane, and next thing you knew, the morsel had become part of him. Now he was coming into contact with the fledgling CEO of Sheraton Hotels. Profitable, reputable, a bit unsettled at the moment, Sheraton made a tempting target, and Geneen was soon striding through the dune grass, paying neighborly calls. He gave Henderson the standard cozening speech: Think of the resources you'll have available. Think of the possibilities for growth. Think of the benefits to the stockholders. And—while this last didn't need to be more than hinted at in the salubrious and genteel salt air of the Cape—think of the dump truck full of money you're going to walk away with. Besides, Geneen assured, the present management, maybe with some minor changes, would be retained to run the new division; ITT respected and would need Henderson's expertise. What ITT was proposing was, in effect, a partnership.

Geneen made his case with exquisite equanimity; to him, it was a business deal, and in fact a rather puny one by his standards. To Henderson, however, it would mean a thorough rewriting of what he thought was the story of his life. He pondered, he agonized. He consulted with his board and agonized some more. Then he decided to sell. "It wasn't what I wanted," he says. "I wanted to keep the company as it was—but I couldn't shake the feeling that that was very selfish of me. I had a responsibility to the shareholders and the employees. It seemed like they would benefit, and I couldn't let my ego stand in the way of that. I did what seemed like the right thing at the time."

In February of 1968, Sheraton was taken over by ITT. Harold Geneen now owned Ernie Henderson's beds, dishes, and ballrooms, and Ernie Henderson now owned a wad of stock in Harold Geneen's empire.

To the casual observer, Ernie Henderson hadn't lost a thing. He was still president of something called Sheraton Hotels, and he had a contract to run the outfit for five years. It took him about two months to realize that he could not work with his new "partner."

"I was a cog," he says, "a flunky. Every month they came in with twenty-three corporate vice-presidents to tell me what to do—not *ask*, not consult with me: *tell* me. Their idea of what the company was bore no resemblance to mine. We'd built a reputation for friendliness and service. We'd paid lousy salaries and everybody knew it, but we had a very loyal staff because we treated people well, we instilled some pride, we functioned as a team. I tried to convince the corporate people that what they'd really bought was the rights to that team; they thought they'd purchased such-and-such amounts of bricks and mortar sitting on such-and-such amounts of real estate."

To provide for orderly succession, Henderson stayed on one year with the new regime. Then he walked. Within two years all but a pair of his twenty-seven top managers from the pre-ITT days were also gone.

Upon leaving Sheraton, Henderson founded a company to establish and operate nursing homes in New England; because of changes in laws pertaining to medical insurance, the business achieved only a moderate size, and he has since passed it on to his daughter. More recently, at the age of sixty, he has bought out a small manufacturing firm that makes eyeglass cases. For diversion, the erstwhile hotelier has worked for more than a decade on a massive genealogy, and has so far identified more than eighteen thousand of his forebears. Since 1969 he has served as Secretary to the Class of '49, writing notes for the alumni bulletin, serving as a clearinghouse of news and gossip, positioned, like Lear, as one of "God's spies," reporting "who loses and who wins, who's in and who's out."

For reasons of pride or some nearly obsolescent sense of gentlemanly form, Henderson will go just so far in complaining about the disposition of his family business and the treatment he received at the hands of ITT. He will say that it was probably a mistake to sell, that he overestimated the strength of his post-sale position. Classmates of his, however, will state his case more strongly. "Ernie got royally screwed," says one. "He's much too nice a guy to go head-to-head with ITT, and he was very naïve about it. There were precedents for what would happen to him, for how a holdover from a family operation would be purged. It was clear that ITT would want him out, and of course it was easy enough for them to drive him crazy. They gave him what he needed least in the world, which was money, and took away what he needed most, which was the shot at finally being boss. They murdered his baby for him, is what it comes down to."

Among the Class of '49, Ernie Henderson stands as the most dramatic victim of what, in the years around the middle sixties, came sweeping in as essentially a brand-new way of doing business in America. He wasn't, however, the only victim.

Back in those years a '49er named Arnie Berlin was the number-two guy and heir apparent at the Chicago Musical Instrument Company, which his father had founded and was still running, and which "probably made the tuba or trombone you played in your high-school band." In 1970 the outfit was scarfed up in an unfriendly takeover by a firm called Ecuadorian Companies, Ltd., whose main products were cement and beer for the South American market. "Cement and beer!" says Berlin, as if the dubious combination astounds him even now. "What they wanted with glockenspiels was a mystery to me. But they did manage to reposition us from being a highly profitable consumer company to a tax loss." Berlin, like Henderson, was driven to resign not long after the takeover.

Then there was a guy named Charley Miller, in his

heart more a scientist than a businessman, who was happily running a sweet little high-tech company that put electrolytic coatings onto metals, when the company suddenly vanished in a merger. "It turned my life upside-down," Miller recalls, "so I told myself, huh-uh, no more high-tech. Too volatile. So next I ended up with the lowest-tech operation I could find. I ran a furniture company. We made dinettes. Do I have to finish the story? That one got swallowed up, too."

So just what the hell was going on out there?

What was going on was nothing short of a profoundly basic change in the strategies that corporations were using to make money. It used to be that they turned a profit by the sale of products and services. Now they were trying to beat the game by the buying, selling, and occasional dismantling of other companies. "Paper entrepreneurialism" this new approach was called. Its tools were the leveraged buy-out, the stock swap, and the so-called creative modes in bookkeeping and tax avoidance, and its appeal lay in its promise—not always fulfilled—of making money without the irksome necessity of actually creating wealth. In style as in substance, paper entrepreneurialism was a slap in the face to virtually every precept, moral or commercial, of the postwar way of doing things. The irony is that it had been the postwar generation that unwittingly paved the way for its ascendance.

Paper entrepreneurialism was dashing, it was sexy, it was mean. Most of all, it was shiny new—as untarnished and credible as modern scientific management had been in 1949. Strange to tell, before 1965 there had been virtually no such thing as an unfriendly corporate takeover in this country. Competing firms were free to try to beat each other's brains out in the marketplace, but as for trying to gobble each other whole and entire, that was beyond the pale of decency. When companies *did* merge, it was because they had something to offer each other in terms of consolidating product lines or making more efficient use of marketing channels.

By the middle of the 1960s all of that was changing. The site of the corporate *mano a mano* was shifting from the marketplace to Wall Street, and companies did battle through the arbitrageurs, fighting not for customers but for controlling blocs of each other's paper; as with contending Dobermans, the game now was to convince the other dog that you could open your jaws wide enough to eat his face. Mergers were no longer based on harmonies in production and marketing, but on balancing acts between profits and losses, capital gains and accelerated depreciation. And mergers happened far more often. Between 1963 and 1967 alone, the number of corporate marriages doubled, and more and more of them were shotgun weddings. By 1981 the unfriendly takeover and the corporate raid had become such staple stratagems that fully 49 percent of the chief financial officers at America's largest industrial firms acknowledged fears that their companies might be targets. The paranoid atmosphere necessarily had its consequences. By 1983, with executive job security at probably the lowest point in fifty years, 30 percent of the country's managers had résumés out at any given time. Hundreds of millions of dollars in stockholders' money was being squandered on nonworking CEOs who'd had the foresight to arrange "golden parachutes" for themselves. The American vocabulary, if not the American economy, was enriched by the introduction of "greenmail" as the big-money guys realized that a bluffed takeover could generate a payday as rich as and far less troublesome than a consummated deal.

The business press dubbed the paper entrepreneurialists a new breed of businessman—and a new breed they largely were. The bulk of them came from financial backgrounds, an unprecedented percentage were lawyers, and virtually none of them had come up by way of the making or selling of goods; the new breed made the final quantum leap in business's abstraction, virtually ignoring the marketplace altogether and going straight to the computer and the tax code in search of profit opportunities.

But a funny thing happens when a new breed is announced: the guys who were setting the tone before, automatically, helplessly, come to be thought of as the *old* breed, a little bit tired, a little bit passé. And as the paper wizards of the sixties and beyond moved to center stage, the men of the postwar, with their short graying sideburns, their college-age kids, their rococo expressions like "gangbusters" and "yea-bo," did indeed seem to have lost their patina of modernity. As individuals they were set, secure, but as a trend-setting group they were beginning to be reacted against, pushed into the wings, where they would watch the new developments with varying degrees of disapproval and chagrin. Weaned on the methodology of Ad Prac, they were no strangers to hardball; under the new rules, however, business was coming more closely to resemble roller derby. A lot of what was going on struck them as nasty, flagrantly self-serving, utterly ahistorical, and just plain wrong.

But why had paper entrepreneurialism come about in the first place? It came about for the same reason that new developments in business *always* come about: because it presented itself as the easiest way to make the most money at a given point in time. And that point in time had been bequeathed to the paper entrepreneurs by the men of the postwar generation.

The business ethos of the fifties and the early sixties had been predicated on a rising living standard and a robust rate of growth. With more people every year able to afford the Acrilan carpet or the Bendix dryer, *of course* the sensible approach to corporate success was to make an appealing widget with a competitive price tag on it—to stake out a piece of the pie, and to profit as the pie itself expanded.

But what if this larger pie stopped growing? What if apparent economic gains were nullified by inflation? What if, because of lapses in quality and lags in productivity, domestic companies started selling proportionately fewer widgets than foreign ones? What if, because of a dearth of innovation, a holding back from *real* entrepreneurship, new jobs failed to materialize and consumer spending couldn't continue to spiral? What if, in short, the generation that flourished under the strategy of growth failed to perpetuate that growth?

In that case, a new strategy—one predicated on stasis or even decadence—would be called for. And that strategy, as the new breed figured out, was paper entrepreneurialism. If the pie wasn't getting bigger, it made less sense to throw in new ingredients than just to try to finagle a bigger slice of what was already there. By deft financial maneuvering, it was discovered, money could be skimmed off without the need of putting anything back in, and as the practice became more general, American business came ever closer to the drear model of the zero-sum game, in which, by definition, someone must be getting screwed if someone else is getting rich. Gone was the climate in which American enterprise could presume to say and maybe even to believe that its constituency was as high and wide as America itself.

The paper entrepreneurialists, then, were something like the bastard offspring of the postwar generation, the evidence of their earlier miscalculations, and while the men of the old breed didn't have to like the men of the new, they couldn't quite deny their lineage either. They certainly couldn't avoid working with them. When they did work together, though, the conflicts in styles and philosophies were sometimes nothing short of epic. Ask John Grant, who in 1969 was hired by American Standard to be a foil to then chairman and grand acquisitor William D. Eberle.

Now, before the onset of the merger and acquisition craze American Standard had been a paradigm of the old-style U.S. manufacturing company. It made a necessary product, generated modest but rock-steady earnings on vast volume and gentlemanly margins, avoided overdiversification as something unwise and debt as something unclean. Those had been the company traditions since 1899, and the firm could boast that its sober philosophy had enabled it to become the acknowledged leader in its field. Everybody knew the American Standard trademark, though most people noticed it only subliminally. The company had made and sold one out of every five toilet bowls in the entire free world.

In the hothouse atmosphere of the middle sixties, however, that sort of staid accomplishment did not excite. The investment community didn't want plumbing, it wanted pizzazz; it didn't want three quarters of a century of proven performance, it wanted the hot rumor in tomorrow's paper, the sudden salacious leap in the stock price.

So American Standard decided to get sexy. In 1966 it turned the whole company ethos upside down by bringing in Eberle, a lawyer who'd built a reputation as an aggressive conglomerate-builder at Boise Cascade. Eberle's mandate was to get out there and buy some growth, and he set about the mission with the wild-eyed glee of a Gurkha. The only problem, as *Fortune* would later observe in parlance whose understatement would bring a smile to the faces of connoisseurs, was that "unfortunately, Eberle was a better acquisitor than strategist." He bought with the insouciant randomness of a Kuwaiti with a six-foot blonde at Tiffany's. Bank safes, railroad brakes—it was all the same to him. What mattered was to move fast and gobble up those quailing little companies before some other hotshot got them; only later could you pause to consider where or if they fit in the overall corporate scheme.

But it was visibility that American Standard had wanted, and "Wild Bill," as he was known to certain colleagues, gave the company its money's worth of that. As the firm's debt went through the roof and its stock price was falling through the floor, AS made the headlines almost every week, over stories that described it, essentially, as the most fantastically bemuddled corporation in America. The directors decided it seemed to be time to bring in someone to try to keep Wild Bill's trigger finger off his wallet.

Enter John Grant, a trim, fastidious, soft-spoken but rather high-strung man whose conservative fiscal bent had been bolstered by ten years in a Philadelphia bank and ten as financial chief of dignified but sluggish Sinclair Oil—itself a takeover victim in 1969. To Grant, Eberle's methods were nothing short of heretical; yet not even he was immune to the undeniable scintillation of the hunt for new properties. "Those were extraordinarily exciting times, even, for a while, euphoric times," he says, by way of explaining his decision to take the job at all. "And though I certainly had some qualms from the beginning, I figured, what the hell, I'd try to keep an open mind and see what these gutsy modern guys were doing."

As it turned out, though, Grant's open mind soon filled up with a blend of incredulity, indignation, and outright horror. "I saw this company from the inside," he says, "and suddenly I began to wonder if maybe it was me, maybe I was losing my marbles. Either everything I'd ever learned was wrong, or something very macabre was going on here. This guy was flitting all over the place, doing back-of-the-envelope acquisitions work—you know, our earnings are a dollar ninety this year, and two thirty next year, and three twenty the year after that, and if we acquire this and that and give 'em this much cash and this much stock, then *they* can earn X-Y-Z and we'll all come out over here. All this scribbled on the back of an envelope, mind you, maybe while he's running to catch the elevator. Man, it was wild.

"But those were the Wallpaper Days," John Grant continues, a slightly perverse nostalgia entering his tone, as when old soldiers tell you about the gruesomest battle they ever saw. "Everybody was printing up preferred this and convertible that and sticking it on their walls, and I watched this company go from thirty million dollars' worth of debt in 1967 to *half a billion* dollars' worth of debt, most of it short-term and expensive as hell, in 1970. By that time we had no money, we couldn't even meet our goddam dividend that year, the banks were closing down on us—and Eberle was *still* out there trying to buy! He was after an Italian air-conditioner company for thirty million. He was buying carpet companies, school learning machines—anything that was out there, we were chasing. And I thought, 'By Christ, this is the wildest thing I've ever seen.' I was financial vice-president—as far as the outside world had any way of knowing, all this was going on with my approval. *My approval?!* I would as soon have given my approval to Armageddon. But I couldn't rein this guy in. He was unleashable. My nerves were shot. I finally said, 'Screw it, I am not going to be associated with this.' I quit."

Grant retreated to his beach house in Quogue, Long Island, while American Standard came closer and closer to flushing itself down its very own toilet. Its stock price, by early '71, had plummeted from the mid-forties to a low of seven—Wall Street's humorous and compassionate way of saying Nice Try on the firm's effort to become the sort of company that Wall Street claimed to love. In courting the Street's favor, American Standard had made itself ridiculous, a fat but stately seventy-year-old matron suddenly playing the coquette. With the firm's reputation besmirched and with bankruptcy looming as a distinct possibility, the board decided that they'd had enough of the brave new world. They booted Eberle, who made an oddly appropriate soft landing by ending up as Richard Nixon's special trade representative. To run the company, they elected William A. Marquard—of all things, an operations guy. And they asked John Grant if he would please come back and, this time, *really* handle the financial side. Together, Marquard and Grant got rid of some of Eberle's more bizarre acquisitions, paid off the short-term debt and restored the company's credit, and stocked the upper-management pond with guys who knew their way around a factory. By early 1984, with the unsexy-again corporation having taken a giant step backward from the frontiers of modernity and souped-up growth, the stock price stood at sixty-six.

John Grant retired in 1983, at the age of sixty, with a five-year contract to hang around American Standard as a consultant and a sort of cautionary presence. Several mornings a week he goes to the grim old company headquarters on 40th Street in Manhattan—a building with a showroom full of bathtubs and bidets at sidewalk level—and settles into his office overlooking Bryant Park, exuding moderation and the slightly distracted serenity of a person who has walked away from an awful wreck and is still musing on the meaning, if any, of his survival.

"Look," he says, "it's not that I don't understand the temptation that this company was facing. We deal in pretty mundane products that already have a hefty market share in industries that are mature. So there's a real temptation to look around at what other guys are doing with this razzle-dazzle high-growth stuff, and to feel that maybe you're missing the boat. It has to do with the mind-set of this whole culture, this idea that high growth is exciting and low growth is for dullards. But what's the growth based on? Is it real growth based on expanding markets or improved productivity? Or is it house-of-cards growth that's spun out of air? Look, as this company found out in spades, growth for the sake of growth is a loser. And it's ridiculous to take that cents-per-share stuff as the only criterion for judging a company's performance. How about stability? How about the virtue of keeping long-term faith with the shareholders and customers? How about simple sanity?"

Grant crosses his hands across his belly, half-swivels toward the window, spends a moment contemplating the treetops of the park. When he turns back toward his desk, his face is that of a man who's just been let down by a friend.

"The part that nettles me," he says, "is that I can't help thinking that the investment community should have known better. *Did* know better. The conglomerate types went on this two-plus-two-equals-five kick, directors didn't have the nerve to call them on their math, and the investment bankers managed to justify thinking that it all made sense. They made money every time somebody cut a deal, after all. They weren't about to get up on a pedestal and say, 'Hey, this isn't a very sound way for the American industrial complex to move.' So they played it like something out of 'The Emperor's New Clothes.' They just kept mum and went along on the sleighride.

"Maybe in better times it wouldn't have seemed so selfish or so smug. There's more slack in better times, I suppose. But this was at a time when the country was getting to be in some very real trouble. This was like taking long luxurious baths when you know the well is running dry. And the worst part was that people seemed proud of what they were getting away with, proud of how clever they were, as if they were saying, 'I can make a lot of money even in an economy going nowhere. Isn't it terrific?'

"Well, no," says John Grant, "it wasn't terrific. It wasn't terrific in the least."

Interlude

What Becomes
a Legend Most?
II

Wine lovers still rhapsodize about the cabernet sauvignon produced in the Napa Valley in 1974. Enormous yet velvety, say the conventional; virile yet searching, say those who strain to be original about such things. Nineteen seventy-four was the year that Napa cabernets beat the hell out of Bordeaux in blind tastings all around the world, as well as the year that zinfandel became respectable.

This may seem like no big deal in the grand scheme of things, but it is at least a way of accentuating the positive: the California vintage was about the only thing that went right for America that year.

Everything else was a fiasco. Nineteen seventy-four was the year in which an American President ingloriously slithered down from office, a year when OPEC was in the first cackling flush of its power and oil prices had recently tripled. Taking a lesson from that other cartel, sugar refiners jacked up their prices by 400 percent that year, and, for good measure, harvest-time hailstorms shredded the produce of the Middle West.

Even logic took a beating in 1974. Keynesian economics had posited the somewhat comforting notion that capitalist economies could be stricken by either the fever of inflation or the cancer of unemployment, but couldn't reasonably die of both at once. Yet, in 1974, 41 percent of U.S. auto workers were laid off, while the United Mine Workers were negotiating a contract that called for a 64-percent increase in wages and benefits. Gerry Ford would soon be sporting a button that said WIN, for Whip Inflation Now, while anticipators of an opposite disaster were wearing pins that said BATH, for Back Again To Hoover. Prices were rising at the highest rate since the brief consumer orgy of 1947, while production was in the longest slump since before the war machine got cranking in 1941. The University of Michigan reported that public confidence in the economy's performance was at by far the lowest point ever in the twenty-four years they'd been doing the survey. The Dow Jones average fell 459 points between January '73 and Christmas '74, ending up where it had stood in 1962, except that a dollar was now worth sixty-one cents; *Time* summed up the mood on Wall Street by observing that "rarely has fear scored so total a victory over greed."

Nineteen seventy-four was the '49ers' silver jubilee, and all in all, a more forlorn atmosphere in which to celebrate a quarter-century of stewardship over American enterprise could hardly be imagined. The U.S. foreign-trade balance had just slipped from surplus to deficit; the first wave of belly-ups among small and midsize businesses had recently started heaving. Every indication was that the big time was over, that the decadence had irreversibly kicked in, that the well had been allowed to get so low that the pump was sucking air.

And yet when *Fortune* magazine again turned its spotlight on the Class of '49, its tone was cheery, deferential, almost embarrassing, really, in its unalloyed enthusiasm. As Harry Figgie would put it, America was in a war and was losing it; oddly, that somehow made it seem like a perfect time to throw a ticker-tape parade for the generals. The troops' morale demanded it.

As did the media's mix, which needed, after all, some good news to intersperse among the bad. By 1974 what was going on with the men of '49 had become not a distillation of, but a vivid counterpoint to what was going on with the country at large. The '49ers by then were out of the scrap, largely impervious to personal setbacks, snug in the realm of the long-term contract, the controlling alliance on the board, and, in certain cases, the golden parachute. In an America where it no longer seemed that most people would make it, the '49ers showed, at least, that those who did would make it big.

Which is to say the emblematic role that *Fortune* had assigned to them fifteen years before had now been stood directly on its head. As young men in a time of optimism and growth, they'd been cast as regular joes, only more so—the friendly eggs in the split-level on the hill, to whose salaries, titles, and self-contentment we might all legitimately aspire. Well, that no longer seemed quite plausible. By 1974 America's promise had become more closely held, and the men of '49 could only be presented as magnificent exceptions, the guys who, stagflation notwithstanding and foreign trade be damned, had broken through to glory. Their role now was to inspire by offering living proof that the game could in fact be beaten, the odds could be licked. In 1974 they were trotted across the stage rather like characters from Homer, salt-and-pepper-haired reminders of a time when heaven and earth were closer together and the gods came down and intervened directly in the affairs of men, making destinies outsized.

They were heroes, these postwar MBAs, they were titans, and their every stratagem and tic now seemed worth examining; who knew where clues to their fulfillment and success might lie? Accordingly, *Fortune* saw fit to report such minutiae as that the typical Class member spent thirty-five minutes a week at concerts but only twenty-seven at sports events, that 51 percent endorsed the Pill but only one in ten was in favor of coed dorms. One percent of the Class of '49 opposed the free-enterprise system, 6 percent strongly favored interracial marriages, and 17 percent modestly averred that their physical appearance had been a great professional advantage. Content as husbands and fathers, only 14 percent of the Class had been through a divorce; more than half had wives who didn't work, though 79 percent gallantly conceded that the little lady had been helpful-to-very-helpful in abetting their own careers. Eighty percent of the Class felt that they had been neither too strict nor too permissive toward their kids; only 21 percent believed their children had experimented with marijuana, and only 4 percent thought their sons and daughters had sampled harder drugs. Socially, in the parlance of Stanley Greenfield, they fell "maybe twenty percent along the urban-culture-vulture-tennis-playing axis, and eighty percent along the subur-

ban-country-club-eighteen-holes-and-dinner-dance axis."
Fifteen percent, at a median age of fifty-one, were grandfa-
thers. If the men of the Class had it to do all over again,
nine out of ten would go back to the Harvard Business
School and do it all just about the same.

Now, as a document, "The Class the Dollars Fell On"
was several things at once. At one level it was simply a
group portrait of some wealthy, middle-aged businessmen.
At another, it could be read as a précis of the MBA mental-
ity, or as a map of where people end up once they fan out
from Soldiers Field. Between the lines, however, the article offered a laconic sketch of the priorities of a generation,
an account of what had mattered in America at the height
of its blustery prowess, according to a highly influential
group certain of its prerogatives and largely unhobbled
by doubt. What it came down to is that the men of '49
hadn't just achieved success, they'd *defined* success. Their
standards became those that people would be measured
against when the question was whether they were meas-
uring up.

Back when they were junior execs, they'd set their
goals in an atmosphere of such remarkable consensus that
characterizations of the American suburbs as a capitalist
utopia were less facetious than sly. The frost-free Frigi-
daire, the wet bar, and the Lionel trains for Johnny in the
finished basement—these were things not only pleasant
in themselves, but evidences of participation in the joyous
drama of an America being carried by Yankee know-how
and burgeoning organizations into a future that had only
forward gears. "To be a part of that"—as Stanley Greenfield had implored at his B School interview—was an all
but universal hope, and the men of Harvard Business '49,

because of their educational advantages and personal talents, went on to be as big a part of it as 652 individuals possibly could. What others yearned for, they accomplished, and having won the game, they of course became staunch defenders of the game. They husbanded the mainstream version of virtue through all its knocks and trials; they made its satisfactions manifest. The life they led became the standard life, the exemplary life, in which you found a niche and worked hard in it, married the right woman at the right time, sent children to good schools, bought insurance and made prudent investments, and retired with enough time to dandle babies and enough money not to be a burden on the young. A comforting circularity held the whole thing together: you knew it would feel good to do it because you knew it was the right thing to do.

Besides, it was a life that produced more than its share of tangible rewards, some of them as primal as the home on high, secure ground, some of them as arbitrary as the sad dry haddock relentlessly dispensed in the mahogany dining rooms of private men's clubs in New York or Philadelphia. But no matter: every society evolves its own system of preferments, and the signs of status could as easily be spears and blankets as corner offices, walnut dashboards, or the effortlessly obtained courtside box or ringside pair of seats. What counts is that the definitions of prestige speak a language that is broadly understood and has the power to set the emulative juices flowing. The whole idea is motivation, and by that criterion the '49ers' version of success has been perhaps the most persuasive that the modern world has seen. Almost everybody wants what they have. Women want it firsthand. Yuppies want it more than sex, dignity, or a good night's sleep. Minorities damn well want their shot at it, and erstwhile radicals slink toward it like flotsam at the outmost fringes of an eddy. Even Chinese Communists want it these days, if you can believe what you read in the papers.

When the specimen '49er, then, drives or is driven home at the end of the day, he travels through a world with a top, a middle, and a bottom, and he has the quiet and almost subliminal pleasure of knowing where he stands. The clues are all around him. Smudged fringes of the city where he makes his money will fall away, giving onto quiescent suburbs where the maples have not been bulldozed and the houses are one-of-a-kind, where the girls still wear pink and the boys learn early that sloops are esthetically and morally superior to motorboats. In the '49er's driveway, gravel will crunch reassuringly under radial tires, and at his front door he will be met by a dog of nonrandom parentage and by a handsome wife, still stylish and well-spoken, who has dealt gracefully with the sadness of the children going off, has kept her daytime drinking within the bounds of politesse, and who does more than her share of good works in the community. His dinner will tend toward the healthfully austere, with white space on the plate between the veal chop and the broccoli, and after eating, if he clings to the Class average, he will watch television for fifty-four minutes and/or read for fifty-five point seven. Before going to sleep, he will almost certainly look at the pictures of his kids, smiling straight-toothed smiles in a triple frame on his bedroom dresser. The oldest, a girl and a real go-getter, the one who always tried the hardest to make him proud of her, will have been among the first females accepted to Princeton or Yale, and now be an associate at a highly regarded law firm in New York. The youngest, the baby, after a stint of brave and torturous indecision, will have made his peace with following in Daddy's footsteps and somewhat tardily enrolled at HBS. And the middle boy, the quiet one, who doesn't call home as often as his parents wish he would, will perhaps have left college after freshman year and be off in Colorado, Tunis, or Alaska, doing something odd. In public the '49er will take special care to say how approving he is of his middle child's unconventionality, and in private he will pray to God he really means it.

As it had been from the start, however, the hard facts that propped up the '49er legend were contained in the numbers, and by 1974 the numbers were stratospheric. The Class's median income of $53,561 (equivalent to roughly 112K in 1985 money) was almost five times the median figure for all American *households,* and was more than triple the typical earnings even of males with five or more years of college. The Class's median net worth—over half a million dollars, updated—placed its members in the top 1 percent of all Americans, even though reckoning by median minimized the influence of the family fortunes and of such conspicuous achievers as Henry Sage, who'd made the current equivalent of $22 million in Brazilian steel, and John S. R. Shad, who was salting away an estimated $16 million as vice-chairman of E. F. Hutton before going public service as Reagan's chairman of the SEC. While the men of '49 had always been optimistic, by 1974 it was abundantly clear that things had turned out even better than they'd dared predict. Upon graduation, they'd estimated that a decade out they'd be earning $12,000 (allowing for inflation), and in fact ended up commanding $14,000; twenty years from the starting gate, they thought their market value would be $24,000 but actually it was $32,500. As for the sort of arithmetic that pertained at the silver jubilee, no one had even dared intone those figures back in 1949.

On the other hand, what people *had* made bold to murmur back at the beginning of the big time was the faith that the billowing American prosperity would be well managed enough to last a long, long time, and vast enough so that virtually everyone could bask in it. The modern American economy would be organized sort of like a gigantic jetliner: there'd be passengers in first class, passengers in coach, and passengers on standby, with people very like the '49ers manning the controls; service wouldn't be exactly equal all around, but at least the altitude of everyone who'd come on board would rise together as the American jumbo flew ever higher. It was a nice idea, but by 1974 it was impossible not to notice that it wasn't quite turning out that way. Real income for the guy in coach was shrinking; the GNP, in constant dollars, was on a slow but palpable descent. For the men of '49, it was more than a little embarrassing. Back in the days of the Postwar Code, they'd set forth, if not exactly with a mission, then at least with the classic pragmatist's assumption that one would do good by doing well. By the time of their silver anniversary, the evidence was all around them that that proposition had turned out to be more convenient than true. History was making them seem more selfish than they were, or at least more selfish than they honestly thought themselves to be.

In 1979 *Fortune* covered the '49ers for what seems to

have been the final time, in an article whose tone was un-
usually informal, anecdotal, autumnal. "Reassessment
Time for the Forty-Niners" the piece was called, and it
contained hardly a single statistic. By '79 the Class had
achieved such a staid gray eminence that the wallet-sniff-
ing would have seemed gauche, and besides, in the mire of
the Carter years, it seemed almost too cruel to remind the
younger hopefuls that people used to make money in this
country. The thirtieth-anniversary dispatch, in fact, could
almost as easily have run in *Psychology Today* as in the
business press. What it dealt with was personal growth
and change, with responses to the prospect of getting old.

In 1979 the '49ers' median age was fifty-six. Some
members of the Class had mandatory retirement looming
up ahead, and were frankly baffled as to how they'd fill
their hours without the ready refuge of a job. Others were
tweaked by questions about the real value of what they'd
done so far, and by quandaries as to what was still worth
doing next. In all, the concerns were pressing enough so
that the Class invited Gail Sheehy, author of *Passages* and
the midwife of the midlife crisis, to speak at its thirtieth reunion. Sheehy lectured them, surveyed them, and later
referred to Class members, with changed names and pre-
sumably in composite form, in her 1981 book, *Pathfinders.*
Quietly, belatedly, with the earnest awkwardness of white
people learning to break-dance, the '49ers were claiming
their slot in the Me Decade; it was the seventies in
America, and the HBS men, too, were going to see to their
own emotional needs.

After lifetimes of deferred gratification and steadfast
cleaving to the norms that they themselves had done so
much to limn, the '49ers, some of them, began to flirt with

self-indulgence. Between 1974 and 1979, at the tail end of careers remarkable for their stability, more than a quarter of the Class changed jobs. A few men retired, several went nonprofit, but the largest number of those who moved went from larger companies to smaller ones—places relatively free of the organizational complexities that the '49ers had once reveled in, relatively stripped of the hierarchies that the postwar MBAs themselves had helped to engineer. After three decades of largely playing it safe and tight, these guys now had a hunger for the fast and loose. Nearly a dozen finally went into business for themselves. The early dreams of being one's own boss, even at the cost of having to make the coffee and lick the stamps, not to mention meet the payroll, were asserting their hold at last. Finally, with the kids through school and the estate pretty well set up, they could afford to acknowledge that maybe the big established corporations weren't where the action and the satisfaction were, after all; maybe there was something irreplaceable about a passion and a risk of one's own. If the realization came too late to infuse the American mainstream with the Class's prime-of-life entrepreneurial energies, it at least allowed the '49ers themselves to exercise aspects of their competence that had been lying dormant since the days of Soldiers Field, when the aim had been not to be a functionary, an intersection in the matrix, but a compleat businessman, a guy who did it all.

Amid this flurry of midlife epiphanies there were several '49ers who turned away from commerce altogether in favor of some personal crusade. Simeon Wooten, formerly a bank president in Fort Lauderdale, became, according to *Fortune,* "worried that the drift toward egalitarianism in the U.S. [was] eroding the foundations of capitalism" and went back to school for a doctorate so that he could spend his autumn years imbuing the young with the righteous fire. Arthur B. Kellogg, who ran his own accounting firm in California, became a pamphleteer for radical tax reform, writing that "we should all be angry enough to resort to physical violence" in response to the abuses of the IRS and in order to get the bulk of the tax burden off the shoulders of wage earners. Connie Jones, contemplating an early retirement that he later decided against, took a year's sabbatical and wrote a book of poetry.

And even among those '49ers for whom nothing had ostensibly changed, 1979 seemed to signal a shift in focus, a turning away from Ad Prac's relentless emphasis on ways and means, toward a consideration of what the whole scramble had really been about. In 1979 Pete McColough was still CEO of Xerox. By then Xerox was floundering and had become about as good a paradigm for American bloat as you could find outside Detroit; still, there it was, all $7+ billion of it, with its universally famous name and its ineradicable place in the history of business. Even so, in 1979 Pete McColough could confide to the public record that "sometimes . . . when I drive home at night . . . I think, really, if Xerox itself completely disappeared tonight . . . basically the world is not going to be very different."

That statement, as it happened, was probably the last word by a '49er in the periodical Class history. It's the line that rings down the curtain on that aspect of the legend, and it does so with the slyly subversive edge that candor almost always has. If Xerox could disappear, why not Bloomingdale's, why not General Dynamics, why not ABC, why not the whole version of America that was perceived and boosted by the Harvard Graduate School of Business Administration? Only because a certain momentum had been established, a certain version of success subscribed to, and too much blood, sweat, and money had been anted up to suddenly change the game. That was really the only reason, when you looked at it hard and ventured past the pieties. Even the Postwar Code—for all its bright-eyed passion and for all the goose-bump-raising rhetoric that went with it—what had it really added up to? It had fallen about seventy-five years short of fostering an American century and an eternity short of husbanding the future. It had fallen about eleven million people short of getting everyone a job, and who knows how many souls short of convincing the world that the U.S. was a force for good. No, as an operative philosophy, the Code had turned out to be just another of those sets of rules that people silently agree to play by, in themselves neither bad nor good. The Code, the phrases, the wild optimism of the long honeymoon and the serene refusal to see the comeuppance looming—at the last, those things just seemed like hugely clever contrivances, resonant and persuasive tricks that a generation had played on itself to get the best out of itself.

They were tricks that worked better than most.

PART III

The View
from
the Top

nine

Tylenol and Other
Headaches

In December of 1982, *Harper's* magazine asked the question: "What could be a worse nightmare for any manufacturer than [having] police patrolling the streets with bullhorns, warning the citizenry that people who use your product are dropping dead?"*

A grimmer prospect is hard to conceive, yet that was the precise situation then confronting one of America's most respected corporations, Johnson & Johnson. Extra-Strength Tylenol, a leading money-maker for that company, was being used as a murder weapon in the Chicago area, and people from coast to coast were being told to flush the product down the john and not buy any more of it. The MO of the still unapprehended killer was simple: he

---

* Michael Kinsley, "Headaches," *Harper's*, p. 20.

(she?) would dump the acetaminophen powder out of a Tylenol capsule, replace it with cyanide, put the capsule back in the bottle and the bottle back on a drugstore shelf, then wait for some random victim to get a headache. Seven people had died after taking the poisoned pills, and there seemed little doubt that the Tylenol brand would follow them to the grave. Clearly, there was nothing wrong with the product itself; still, those capsules had developed an image problem the likes of which had not been seen since Bon Vivant vichyssoise started being equated in the public mind with botulism.

There was a bleak logic in all of this, since the extraordinary previous success of Tylenol had been based on nothing *but* image. Acetaminophen is a widely available aspirin substitute, and is the exact same stuff whether it is contained in a no-frills package or presented, at as much as ten times the cost, under the glossy banner of a brand name. Still, so impressed was the American public with the confident and copious advertising of McNeil Consumer Products (the J&J subsidiary that manufactures Tylenol), and so ingrained was its faith in the parent company, which had brought the world the beneficences of Band-Aids and Baby Oil, that Tylenol, before the murders, owned a spectacular 37 percent of the billion-dollar over-the-counter analgesic market.

Moreover, Tylenol had managed to trump its own ace by making the leap from "Regular-Strength" to "Extra-Strength," and by upgrading its lowly tablet status to the seriousness and dignity of a capsule. The capsule format significantly increased what the analysts refer to as "revenues per headache." It also created a sort of aristocracy of the throbbing temple; "Extra-Strength" was the painkiller of choice for those really high-rent stresses, those agonies that correlated with important problems for important people. You knew it was for real because it looked like something you could only get from a doctor. But, as *Harper's* went on to point out, "there was no medical reason for . . . marketing Extra-Strength Tylenol as a capsule . . . rather than the traditional (and tamper-proof) tablet. . . . Those who live by image shall perish by image."

In the aftermath of the Chicago deaths, J&J put out a nationwide product recall that cost a pretax $100 million. When they put freshly manufactured Tylenol on the shelves, the stuff tended to stay there; Tylenol's market share plummeted to a low of 4 percent, and J&J's market-research findings were not cheery. More than six out of ten former Extra-Strength users said they would probably not go back to the brand, and fully half said that their new aversion extended to the tablets as well. The lawyers started figuring out how much of the debacle could be written off. Concept people at J&J were already trying to think of a snappy name for a new acetaminophen product, to be introduced after this god-awful mess had blown over.

As of late 1984, Tylenol sales were approximately 95 percent of what they were before the murders, and the brand's rescue had already entered the folklore and the casebook. Jim Burke, J&J's chairman and the architect of the turnaround, was being thought of as a bit of a miracle man and a bit of a folk hero. It wasn't just that he'd saved the product; it was that he'd done it by pulling off perhaps the hardest trick of all for a contemporary American CEO: he'd managed to get the public on his side.

This he did, essentially, by refusing to follow the sound, conservative advice he got from almost everyone around him. There were those who wanted to tank Tylenol immediately, lest its stigma spread to other J&J products. There were those who wanted to walk the fence, taking the public pulse before deciding if the brand was worth the continued risk of corporate prestige. Burke decided early that the company would stand by Tylenol, period; he gave the public credit for understanding that the brand itself was not at fault. The FBI counseled against a full-scale recall of the product, seeing it as such an expensive capitulation that it might encourage other cranks; Burke insisted, first of all, that that was a less immediate danger than the possibility of there being more cyanide on the shelves, and, second, that his company could not afford to do anything less than demonstrate total, cost-ignoring concern for the public's safety.

Most dramatically, however, Burke defied the conventional wisdom in his handling of the media. The presumed experts did not want an unstudied executive suddenly facing the interviewers and the cameras. What was to be gained? What could he say that could not be more safely communicated in a well-thought-out, checked and double-checked release—a release that no one could question on the spot? Put him on the tube, give him to the newspapers, and the press would eat him alive. The presumption was that the adversarial relationships among big business, the media, and the consuming public had become so truculent that Burke would inevitably be cast as a target for people's shock and outrage, a stand-in, almost, for the murderer.

Burke saw it differently. Electronic media or no electronic media, there was still a basic, primal, disarming wallop in getting up there in the flesh and showing oneself

to one's accusers. So they'd throw delicate questions at
him—so what? So maybe he'd perspire on camera or show
an instant's lack of poise—who cared? It wasn't a time for
faceless communiqués vetted by a gang of lawyers, and it
wasn't a time to worry about being slick. It was a time,
rather, to allay public anger by confronting it, to let people
know that the company felt as victimized and violated as
they did.

Accordingly, in the days following the first deaths,
when network news was devoting as much as 20 percent
of its air time to Tylenol, there was Jim Burke, making
statements and answering questions, squinting slightly
but not frazzling under the lights, a picture of accountabil-
ity in steel-gray hair, quick blue eyes, and a hearty Irish-
pink complexion. His words were measured but not over-
rehearsed, and he forestalled blame by the simple means
of showing real concern. He made himself available to
everyone. He exposed himself to a grilling on "60 Minutes." He did the Donahue show. He did a news conference broadcast by satellite. He wrote an article for the
Chicago *Sun-Times* that went on to be syndicated nationally. For a time Jim Burke was by far the most visible businessman in America; he'd had perhaps a more
concentrated dose of public scrutiny than any other active
corporate boss ever.

And without exactly trying to, he emerged from the
media blitz as a crusader with an agenda far broader than
the mere redemption of a brand of headache pills. Jim
Burke had become a one-man campaign for the rescue of
the image of big business in America.

The heart of his Tylenol spiel had been a plea for trust,
cooperation, conciliation. His message, ultimately, was

that all of us—the $6 billion multinational just like the yegg with too many babies and too many bills—were floating downstream on the very same raft, subject to the same dangers, the same moments of infuriating helplessness, and that therefore we should all lean together to make the ride go smoothly. It was a message so simple, and delivered in such a homey, cozy style, that it was easy to overlook the fact that, in timing if not in substance, the notion was actually rather bizarre. It was, after all, the heyday of the special-interest group, the treble-damages lawsuit, and the watchdog organization. It was a time when spillage of toxic wastes was causing the evacuation of entire towns, and defense contractors were routinely getting snagged for robbing the taxpayers blind. The AT&T monopoly was finally being broken up, Exxon was being zapped with the biggest price-fixing penalty in history, and here was Jimmy Burke asking the American people to think of big business not as a necessary evil or even a neutral feature on the landscape, but as their friend. If Americans had *ever* thought of big business that way, they certainly hadn't for the last couple of decades or so.

In 1949 it had been different, though exactly *how* different depends on who you ask. Forty-niner John Matthews, who stayed on to teach at the Business School, remembers the immediate postwar years as "a time when the country was very proud of itself, and especially proud of those institutions that had contributed directly to the war effort. The business community certainly shared in the glory." Still, even at that moment of peak solidarity, the image of business was equivocal enough so that when one of the era's most influential executives was asked to speak at the Commencement exercises of the Class of '49, he chose as his subject "the low estate in which we businessmen find ourselves before our employees and the public."

The speaker's name was Lemuel Boulware. He was a vice-president in charge of labor relations and public relations at General Electric, and a distinctive enough figure on the national scene to have had an -ism named for him. Boulwarism, in brief, was an approach to the labor-management dance in which negotiations would be done away with. Instead, management would make public disclosure of a company's earnings, expenses, and forecasts, leading to a rationally determined (i.e., management-determined) and publicly announced contract offer that the rank and file could then take or leave. In Boulwarism's classical model, a company's workers would accept the offer either because it was bound to be fair, or because they knew that there were plenty of other guys who would.

But if Boulware's labor theories smacked of the medieval, his appraisal of how business was perceived was absolutely current, and his remarks to the Class of '49 were of the good-news/bad-news variety. "Here we are," he observed, "with incredible achievements to show for our management of the business side of our wonderful system of freedoms, incentives, and competition. . . . We are phenomenal manufacturers. We have been fabulous financiers. We are superb at individual selling and mass marketing. . . .

"But taken as the whole man of business, each of us is too likely to be condemned by a majority of the public as anti-social. We always seem to be coldly against everything—never seem to know clearly what are the good objectives we *claim* to be seeking . . . [Boulware's italics].

"As a result, too many of our employees and too many of their friends and representatives—in unions, in government, among educators and clergy, in the whole public . . . not only do not respect us but also do not like us. They do not understand or appreciate what we are trying to do. And let's be frank about it—there are times when it looks like *we* don't, either."

Thus the situation could be described in 1949, and by and large it has only gotten hairier in the intervening years. Through the flush fifties, business was too busy making money to take time out to wonder if it was making any friends, and the media began moving toward an increasingly cautionary stance toward what they saw as the monolithic self-concern of major corporations. Perhaps unintentionally, President Eisenhower, in 1956, gave the business community a black eye with his famous coinage of the term "military-industrial complex." The big money was now in league, in the public imagination, with the scariest and most unaccountable sort of power, and the combination seemed sinister and lawless enough so that even now there are people who will confidently assert that it was Big Business that had John Kennedy bumped off. By the end of the sixties, business's bad rep had spread far beyond those partial to conspiracy theories. Business had embarrassed itself by its stands on virtually all the major issues of the time. The big corporations, in the then dominant view, had been grudging if not obdurate on civil rights, blindly gung-ho and then ingloriously waffling on Vietnam. By the early seventies, business was also portrayed as unfair to women, nasty to trees, and loathsome enough to pay Third World people to get pregnant so that hair conditioner could be made from their placentas. In those years, according to Peter Cohen in *The Gospel According to the Harvard Business School,* graduates from Harvard's other divisions would stomp the bleachers, hiss, boo, raise their fists, and make momentous farting noises when the MBA laureates were announced. The line on MBAs was that they were a bunch of short-haired nerds who might be bright but who lacked some animating, humanizing spark, and whose place in the larger scheme would be the performance of those remunerative but joyless tasks that were beneath the engagement of more creative or committed minds. And that's when the economy was *good.*

By the mid-seventies, with the economy going sour, the criticisms of business underwent a subtle but definite shift. Condescension replaced outrage as the dominant tone, and the guys running the show were now presented less as knaves than fools. *Effective* amorality and narrowness you could at least respect; but now these rough-and-ready pragmatists, these action guys, were going right down the tubes. Gigantic corporations were crying for the government to bail them out. Two-fisted free-marketeers, to whom competition had been sacrosanct as long as they were winning, wanted tariff and quota protection all of a sudden. By the early eighties the image of the American businessman was that of the classic bully, beating his chest when the going was easy, screaming for Mama when the going got tough. Not only did the American man of affairs no longer come across as larger than life, he was becoming, in popular portrayals, smaller than life, a " 'bad guy' . . . smirking, scheming, cheating, and conniving

[his] way across the nation's television screens and the pages of its novels."*

This, then, was the background against which Jim Burke was broadcasting his plea for goodwill and pulling together. It was, as he himself acknowledges, a somewhat quixotic undertaking. Still, it was a pitch worth making, and there was no one more perfectly cast to make it than James E. Burke, of Rutland, Vermont. The outlines of his career and life were eloquent testimony that sometimes, at least, the system worked, was responsive to change, and fundamentally benign.

Son of a well-to-do insurance man, Burke had had a classic small-town American boyhood, with solid family and religious values leavened by a salubrious admixture of mischief, sport, and blood. He spent his days around "guns, dogs, and beat-up old cars that we used to hide in the woods before we were old enough to drive." He was an inquisitive but not a studious kid, and barely finessed his way into Holy Cross College, in Worcester, Massachusetts, where he flunked trig and disembarked from French. But the lay brothers of Holy Cross also exposed him to Scotus and Aquinas, and in the searing imperatives of Scholastic philosophy he found a durable ethic that could be wedded to practical activity in an imperfect world. After the Navy and the Business School—to which he would almost certainly not have been accepted had today's grades-and-test-scores admissions criteria been in effect—he became a soap salesman at Procter and Gamble.

It was at P&G that Burke's conscience and the sys-

---

* "The Businessman as Villain," *The New York Times,* April 15, 1984, Business Section, p. 15.

tem's flexibility were first put mutually to the test. The Procter sales philosophy, as Burke tells it, "was a 'load-the-tray' approach—make sure they buy the whole line, and make sure your stuff got put at eye level. It was a power play, as I saw it, and it pressed the line in terms of what I thought was decent, even ethical." Burke was uneasy enough with this offer-you-can't-refuse technique to consider quitting Procter, but stayed on the advice of his father. "First you've got to prove that you can do it their way," the older man advised him. "Then you've earned the right to suggest that maybe they should try it *your* way." So, cleaving to the difficult notion of moral action in a fallen world, Burke hunkered down, sold large amounts of soap, and in fact later had a hand in persuading Procter to ease up on its hard-sell practices.

By 1953, however, Burke was hankering to come back east, and landed a job as a product director with Johnson & Johnson. He settled into Manhattan and reverse-commuted to New Brunswick, New Jersey, but after a year he was antsy to move again. J&J, he felt, "was asleep." It was essentially a nineteenth-century family business which, like the novel *Buddenbrooks,* had survived by virtue of sheer glacial bulk into an era where it didn't quite belong. A fortune big enough to last for many generations had been amassed by the sale of cotton balls and preventive medicine for diaper rash, but what had J&J done lately? Very little, and year after year Johnson & Johnson, by almost imperceptible gradations, had been losing market share on nearly all its products. The Johnsons themselves seemed utterly baffled as to what to do about it, and in fact they didn't particularly seem to care, which drove Jim Burke bananas. In 1954 he quit.

Or rather, he tried to quit. J&J parried his resignation with a 20-percent pay raise and a request that Burke simply sit home in his New York apartment and jot down his thoughts about what was wrong with the company and how it might be put to rights.

So Burke did his analysis, telling the Johnsons, among other things, that they really had to start thinking in terms of new launches to bolster the inevitably stagnating or shrinking revenues from the old warhorses that were the heart of the company's business. Upper management took the suggestion to heart, and by the following year had established a new-products division, with Jim Burke as the head of it. New products, in turn, soon became the hot spot of the organization, and Burke began a measured ascent that would bring him to the chairmanship in 1976. Over the course of his three decades at J&J, he's done more than any other single person to haul the sleeping giant of New Brunswick into the twentieth century; but that, everything being relative, was the easy part. The hard part was doing it without *un*doing the family-values culture that had built the company in the first place—and this Burke seems to have accomplished to an impressive extent. Old General Johnson's Creed—a manifesto of corporate responsibilities and goals—is still promulgated as the company bible, and Burke's own summary of what made the Tylenol rescue possible is "not that we did anything dazzling or clever, but just that we are a company that tries to do the right thing."

Still, in spite of Burke's victory in the battle of Tylenol, the larger war for the image of business seems to be going nowhere, and Burke's frustration shows when he discusses it. "This much is certainly true," he says, sitting in his office at J&J headquarters, overlooking the Raritan River. Burke doesn't use a desk. He decided early on that the only way to triumph over his instinctive sloppiness was to work at a big empty conference table and have his secretary bring him one piece of paper at a time. The table would easily seat a dozen, and sitting at it alone, he resembles a slightly nervous host whose guests are late showing up for the party. "Business in this country serves its various constituencies better than business any-where else in the world—and that includes Japan. The problem is, we just haven't done a very good job of con-vincing the public of that. Other groups—politicians, the media—do a much better job of pointing out what busi-ness does wrong than we do of explaining what business does right.

"Lately," he continues, "there seems to be a bit of a push on. Companies are doing more image ads on televi-sion and in print, and I think that's all to the good. There's a less relentless emphasis on saying Buy Our Product, and a greater recognition of the importance of saying Here's Who We Are. Still, I'm not at all sure that the message is really filtering through at the grass-roots level."

Though there's a distinction, of course, between hav-ing the message filter through and having people *believe* the message, and Burke acknowledges that the man in the street tends to be skeptical of business cheerleading con-ceived, produced, and paid for by business itself.

"Talk about business," he concedes, "and you're talk-ing about profit, which means you're talking about a situ-ation in which not everybody shares equally. Ideally, everybody benefits, but not in the same way. It's an abso-lutely basic tenet of capitalism that the investor is entitled to a fair return on his investment. But let's face it—a lot of people out there don't in their guts believe that an investment of dollars means anywhere near as much as an investment of labor and time, and they resent it when things cost more or whatever so that the shareholders can collect a dividend. Profit—the word, I mean—is an immediate turnoff, it blocks people's minds. And that's a problem."

It's a problem that may very well be eternal. In any case, it hasn't so far been solved by Jim Burke's rapport with the media, or by his speeches to the Ad Council, or by his efforts in Washington with the Business Roundtable. The adversarial climate remains snugly socked in over America. Ralph Nader has not decided to throw in the towel, the FDA has not resolved to leave product safety to the consciences of corporations, and the unions have not come around to thinking that Lemuel Boulware had the right idea back in 1949. Far from all pulling together, the various constituencies of American enterprise remain bent on mutual vigilance so that nobody pulls a fast one.

"You know," says Burke, "even in the response to our handling of Tylenol, there were things I found discouraging. All we did was what we thought any responsible company would have done in our position—and people reacted as if this were some radical new departure for American business. My God, what did people *expect* we'd do? The amount of mistrust and cynicism out there is really depressing.

"So OK, we saved the brand, and we feel very good about that. It meant a lot of money and, more important, provided what I hope is a useful lesson. But beyond that, what's really changed? Labor still says business is bad.

The liberal press still says business is bad. Business says that labor is impossible, the media are irresponsible, Congress is inept, and even the President is letting us down. So no wonder nothing gets done around here."

It's enough to give a guy a headache.

ten

Business Ethics
and the Weather

If Jim Burke was ostensibly concerned with the business
community's public face, there has also been, in recent
years, a heightening concern with business's moral in-
nards—with the internal processes, as it were, that give
business its complexion. Since the late seventies, in fact,
business ethics has seemed to be about as ubiquitous a
topic of conversation as the weather, and has been com-
mented upon to roughly equivalent effect.

In 1977, for example, the *Harvard Business Review*
ran an enormous and scrupulously researched article on
the subject. The study was based on an extensive ques-
tionnaire devised by expert pollsters and answered by
1,227 businessmen. The analysis of the data sprawled
across fifteen pages of the magazine, included seven
charts and six graphs, and cited numerous precedents and

outside authorities. What this massive exercise was leading up to was the bold new insight that "apparently," in
the actual practices of business, "economic values over-
ride ethical values."

One might have thought that conclusion definitive,
but no, the studies and commentaries continued spewing
forth. Another survey, done in 1979, reported that fully 73
percent of American firms had adopted some sort of formal
ethical code, up from 42 percent in 1966. It was also reported, however, that less than half those firms bothered
to distribute codes to their employees, and only 19 percent
of executives believed the codes would raise ethical standards anyway.

Nor was business academia itself exempt from the
probings of moral scrutiny. In 1979 again, Harvard University President Derek Bok, in a quietly but ranklingly
controversial annual report, raised questions about the
Business School's methods and priorities which, according
to *Fortune,* left "even the ethical quality of its instruction
open to doubt."

That doubt might have been more easily dispelled
were it not for a much discussed front-page *Wall Street
Journal* article that had appeared earlier the same year.
The item was entitled "To Some at Harvard, Telling Lies
Becomes a Matter of Course," and it reported how future
MBAs were taught the value of "strategic misrepresenta-
tion." The stink about that one had barely died down by
1982, at which point the B School's moral tone was again
dragged onto the carpet in response to a highly publicized
case of "industrial espionage." In the context of a com-
puter-simulated "business game," one "company" succeeded in accessing another's secret files and blithely used

the pilfered data to drive the competition into the red. Nor did the computer bandits feel that they were doing anything beyond the pale of business-as-usual. Said one: "I thought part of the fun was doing things like espionage or collusion."

By 1984, in a public-relations counterattack, the Business School was doing all it could to call attention to the fact that it offered an entire course on Ethics. Less publicized were such details as that the course was an elective, that it was taken by only 10–15 percent of all MBA candidates, and that it was substantially less heavily subscribed than another B School offering called Power and Influence.

But if ethics had gotten to be a subject that neither companies nor business schools could afford to pass over in silence, the precise meaning of the noises being made resisted coming clear. One *invoked* ethics; one didn't need to *explain* ethics. Ethics had become a buzzword, and as early as 1981 Peter Drucker, writing in *Forbes,* had set about debunking what he saw as the "ethical chic" around him. "Business ethics is to ethics," he observed, "[as] soft porn is to . . . love. . . . Business ethics . . . indeed might be considered more a media event than philosophy or morals."

To at least one member of the Class of '49, however, business ethics was more than all of that combined. For John Matthews, business ethics was business itself, and questions about the discipline's academic legitimacy and the degree of its effectiveness in shaping the behavior of real-world managers were the questions on which the value of his whole life's work would stand or fall. John Matthews had sort of invented the field.

He'd come to Harvard in 1947 and, except for a brief stint as a consultant to the Air Force during the Korean War, he never left. After graduation he stayed on as a research assistant; by 1953 he was teaching. He wasn't teaching ethics yet, for the simple reason that the Business School had yet to come to terms with the handling of the subject, and in fact Matthews' classroom career parallels much of the long and rather confused travail by which the study of business morality finally groped its way onto the B School syllabus.

"Since the late Twenties," a senior faculty member had acknowledged to *Fortune* back in '79, ". . . the subject of ethics . . . has been a struggle for us. . . . It hasn't flourished." As of '53, the closest thing to a formal approach to the topic lay in a course called Business Responsibilities in American Society—BRAS for short—and it was there that Matthews started teaching. As it turned out, however, the course title, like most course titles, was misleading. "It was half macroeconomics, half how to be smart about antitrust," Matthews recalls. "I don't think it ever really came clear what the responsibilities part was about."

After a brief detour into the department of Marketing, Matthews delved again into the School's more theoretical reaches, this time in a course called Business Policy. Insofar as Harvard MBAs are either marveled at or excoriated for thinking like CEOs from their first day on the job, BP has been a big part of the reason why; Business Policy deals with decisions of the sort that are made nowhere but at the very top. In theory, those decisions necessarily had an ethical component; in practice, however, the dilemmas' moral content seemed to be muted by more pragmatic concerns, and by the early sixties, with the time's increasing emphasis on social awareness, it was decided that the voice of conscience needed to be made to speak a little louder, or at least to be given a hearing when other voices were hushed. Before the decade was out, a Social Responsibility module had been added to the Business Policy course; John Matthews taught it.

The problem with a module, however, is that it *was* a module—separate, detachable, overlookable. The message it seemed to send was that ethics, like a caboose on a train, would lend a sweet symmetrical touch to business, but that the locomotive would haul just as well without it. Arguably, at least in the view of conservative theorists like Milton Friedman, that message happened to be 100 percent accurate. Still, it was not a message that America's most visible business school could afford to send at a time when the last vestiges of national consensus were disappearing, when even a Republican President would soon be slapping regulations all over the economy, and when public skepticism toward business was reaching a crescendo. "By the mid-seventies," John Matthews recalls, "we'd begun to wonder—in light of Vietnam, of Kent State, of what had happened in the Nixon administration, in light of the so-called corporate Watergate having to do with payments overseas, which were questionable, and payments to political campaigns, which were illegal—we'd begun to wonder whether we, as an institution, should reexamine what we'd been doing, and ask ourselves if it was enough. We decided it wasn't."

In 1976, after sixty-eight years of turning out leaders for American enterprise, the Harvard Business School, for the first time ever, offered a full-semester course explicitly devoted to the study of business morality. Ethical Aspects of Corporate Policy, it was called, and it was team-taught by Matthews himself and by a young moral-philosophy professor on loan from the Divinity School. The juxtaposition, while sincerely conceived, had something irredeemably quaint about it. One pictures the young moralist crossing the Anderson Bridge with a pulse-quickening mixture of trepidation and zeal, playing missionary to the worshipers of Mammon on the south bank of the Charles; one imagines the executives-to-be taking furtive glances at their Seikos while the ecstatic lecturer held forth on Plotinus, Spinoza, and Mill. In any case, the team approach turned out not to work. Just like they'd told Herb Shayne back in 1947, the place for the abstract consideration of intellectual niceties lay on the Cambridge side of the river; if ethics was to be made palatable to the Business School mainstream at all, it would have to be taught not by precept but by object lesson, and with a view not toward the eternal verities but toward the particular concerns of the commercial mind; it would have to be worked into the case-study format.

Accordingly, in 1980, the Business School hired two young philosophers to write cases, thereby making John Matthews the grand old man in an ethics faculty that had suddenly grown to three. Since 1983 Matthews has moved away from teaching MBAs, confining his classroom activities to the B School's Advanced Management Program.

"What we're trying to do here," he says, "is get across the idea of corporations as 'moral environments.' There's a two-way street about that. Obviously, the tone of the corporation is set by the people running it, but it's also true that what goes on inside a company has an impact on the self-worth, self-image, and dignity of the individual executive. A good team does good things for its players, a bad team does bad things for its players. Either way, it rubs off. We try to prepare people to run good teams."

Matthews' use of the institutional we, it would seem, is one of those unconscious tics that accumulate over a lifetime of teaching. There are others. Many of his remarks end up being questions. He speaks far more slowly and chooses his words with greater care than do most of his former classmates, who tend to rattle off thoughts in the blunt staccato of the business letter. He is gentle in manner, patient in his midwifery of other people's thoughts; yet at the same time there is in his tone a slight defensiveness, a somewhat grudging recognition that the Business School is still academia, the case method is still pedagogy, and the gulf between the rhetoric that rings in the classroom and the bottom-line concerns of real-life business may or may not be bridged by his efforts.

"We can't make saints out of sinners," he says, "and I'm not going to sit here and tell you that every American businessman or every graduate of this school is as honest as he could or should be. Sure, there are crooks out there. But what's happening is that things are moving in a few directions at once. There's no denying that the prestige of business in the eyes of the general public has deteriorated over the last number of years. Unfortunately, though, the same can be said about virtually every institution that we can think of. The church, the university, government— they've all lost credibility. On the other hand, can you really make a case that the general ethical level of business today *isn't* higher than in the days of the robber barons or of the great price-fixing scandals?"

It's a bedeviling question, this issue of relative ethical norms. As with crime rates, the apparent rise or fall tends to have as much to do with how closely people are looking at a given time as with how many no-nos are actually being committed. Besides, one generation's testing of the limits has a way of becoming the next generation's standard accounting practices, while on the other hand, certain new developments in business have started off being hailed as brilliant innovations and ended up being redefined as felonies as their deeper implications emerged. As the more egregious wrongs are identified, mobilized against, and finally put under the rubric of law rather than morality, a whole new set of ethical gray areas emerges.

By consensus of the Class of '49, however, the ethical tone that pertains in the 1980s has gotten lower rather than higher, in comparison with that of the immediate postwar years. The reasons for this are several. A team that's winning easily doesn't have to cheat, and through the heart of the big time, American businesses were romping; when the going gets tough, on the other hand, the tough get gouging. If the tough have computer expertise, access to money-laundering havens, and other such new or expanding appurtenances of white-collar malfeasance at their disposal, so much the better. But the deeper reason for the broadly perceived crisis in business ethics may have less to do with business *per se* than with the fragmentation of the social context in which business has its being. America may or may not have been a moral place in 1949. It seems to have *felt* more moral, though, because the nation's Postwar Code suggested a certain communality-in-spite-of-itself that provided a strong incentive for doing right.

On the surface, of course, America's postwar ethos, far from being collectivist, was the purest distillation of the credo of free enterprise. Individual opportunity, the salutary effects of competition, the fertile Darwinian chemistry of 150 million versions of self-interest colliding—those were the keynotes of the orthodox morality, and with the Cold War heating up, they *had* to be. The Commies had their system, we had ours; it was patriotic to assert and even exaggerate the differences between the two, and it would have been vaguely subversive to suggest that they might have had any similarities at all.

In fact, however, the America of that day had an inclusive notion of itself that, except for the overlay of ideology, was not so very different from that of any other tribe. America had a flag, a mythology, and a mission. The mission, by its very nature, was essentially communal: to foster such a golden age of peace and plenty, a living standard so universally high and wholesome, that, in accordance with the notion of grace made manifest, the whole world would realize we were *right*. America would fulfill its promise not by turning out a million millionaires—that was the easy part—but by providing *everybody* with a polio shot, a supply of Keds and Levi's, and two weeks' paid vacation. Our national glory—and the day's editorial writers did elaborate dances to get this point across without ever sounding socialistic—lay in our promotion of the common weal; a crime against the common weal, in the name of business expediency or anything else, was thought of as a very real crime.

But it would be a mistake born of nostalgia to assume that the years immediately following World War II were an absolute heyday of moral rectitude. If there were fewer scandals, there was also less vigilance; public trust afforded industry a considerable degree of slack. If business seemed less grudging and self-serving in its token nods to social issues, there were fewer social issues to nod to. Jobs were not yet disappearing. The environment was still seen as something you couldn't hurt, and blacks and women weren't really seen at all. If there were fewer lawsuits relating to dubious business practices, it was at least partly because there were simply fewer lawyers looking for something to do.

And if fewer ethical dilemmas seemed to be lying in ambush for the businessman of that time, it was at least partly because that businessman wasn't necessarily geared to think in terms of ethical dilemmas. He hadn't been given the vocabulary for it. It wasn't among the day's preoccupations, either at company headquarters or in the academy. As mentioned earlier, the sole ethical teachings dispensed to the Class of '49 were contained in a course called Public Relations and Responsibilities, in which the emphasis was clearly on the former. Moral issues called forth the slippery vague language that made everybody nervous, and they therefore tended not to hold the floor for long.

It wasn't that people didn't care about the subject. Rather, the scant attention paid to ethics was justified, as '49er Roger Sonnabend recalls, "by the convenient assumption that we all had high ethical standards to begin with, and that *of course* we'd all apply them automatically to business, and *of course* the world of business wouldn't have it any other way. The rules didn't need to be made explicit because good behavior was assumed. Which was fine in theory. But the problem was that in practice there was an uncomfortably thin line between making those quite sincere assumptions, and just signing on with this conspiracy of silence, just going along with the gentlemen's agreement that certain things you didn't talk about."

Such gentlemen's agreements have never sat well with Sonnabend. Shortly after he took over the management of his family's Sonesta Hotels chain in 1951, that company became the first to flout the unwritten rule against having blacks working the front desk or holding other positions where they represented the company to the public. In genteel Boston, where Sonesta is based, Sonnabend has ruffled the calm of his business peers by protesting the anti-Semitic admissions practices of their old-line private clubs. In the Vietnam era, when the business community at large took the safe position of no position, Sonnabend was outspoken and visible enough to earn a spot on Richard Nixon's "enemies list."

Back in 1949, when Sonnabend emerged from Harvard Business School, freshly scrubbed and unashamedly naïve, the discreet silences he found had to do with "entrenched patterns of corruption that were quietly accepted by virtually the whole hotel industry. Owners paid their chefs terribly and got away with it because everybody knew the real money was in the kickbacks the chefs would get from the purveyors. Beverage people got their payoffs, inspectors got their bribes.

"In other industries," he continues, "analogous things went on. Insider trading, for example. In theory it absolutely wasn't done, in practice there seemed no harm in the occasional tip to your mother-in-law or a guy you owed a favor to. Or in situations where you represented a client company—in theory you always put the company's interest before your own, but in the midst of a hard, cold New York winter a junket to the Caribbean could be a real temptation. Let's face it, the stuff existed.

"I was determined," says Sonnabend, "that my company would not be run like that. For me, it was largely an esthetic judgment—I thought it was ugly, misshapen. But I came out of the Business School with no practical framework for dealing with, or even really thinking about, what I saw. You know what it was like? It was like a family that's too bashful or too misguidedly proper to teach its kids the facts of life, so they learn about sex on the street. I learned. I guess we all learned. But if we'd had what was supposedly a practical, no-nonsense business education, why did we have to wait till it hit us in the face before we knew about it?"

Freud theorized that the development of conscience has to do with the internalization of the real or perceived dictates of the mother and the father. For Marvin Traub, however, conscience has to do with the internalization of page one of *The New York Times*.

"That's what I think about," he says, "whenever I have a delicate decision to make. How would it look in big letters on the front page of the morning edition, being read over toast and coffee by customers, colleagues, and friends? That may not be the profoundest motivation, but it's effective."

The method's effectiveness is proportional to how unpleasant it is when something dubious *does* make the papers. Lester Crown, for example, likens the experience to "being boiled in oil." That being the case, Crown must feel quite thoroughly sautéed by now.

Back in 1974 he took the heat in regard to an escapade in which a number of Illinois state legislators were convicted of taking bribes from the coffers of the Material Service Corporation in exchange for supporting a law that would allow heavier cement trucks to thunder along the state's highways. To this day Crown maintains that, while he knew of the money changing hands, he thought it was being used for legitimate campaign contributions, and by the time he learned what it was really going for, everybody was pregnant. Still, it looked bad enough at the time so that Crown's attorneys arranged to have him turn state's evidence in exchange for immunity from prosecution. The upshot, as encapsulated by Chicago columnist Mike Royko, was that "Lester and his button-down flunkies became stoolies [and] went back to the business of getting richer," while the fall was taken by "the two-bit cigar chompers" who'd accepted payoffs of, in some cases, less than two hundred dollars.

Nor did the jailing of those who took the bribes lay the episode to rest. Allegations of further payoffs in connection with Crown's immunity, while never legally pursued, carried enough credibility to figure prominently in the following gubernatorial election. A coda to the story was provided in 1981, when Material Service was accused of bilking the city of Chicago out of $100 million worth of gravel; again, the allegation went unpursued.

But the capers in and around Windy City have been small beer in comparison with alleged scams recently laid at the door of General Dynamics—the nation's third-largest defense contractor, of which the Crown family owns 23 percent currently valued at $892 million, and where Lester is an executive vice-president and the most powerful member of the board.

So complex are the various accusations being leveled against GD that several books are being written on the subject even as the melodrama continues to unfold. Briefly, however, what is being uncovered is a cynical pattern of misbilling and overbilling which runs the gamut from the petty to the gargantuan, which has cost the American taxpayer billions of dollars, and which has seriously undermined the credibility of the Pentagon's entire procurement system. It has been revealed, for example, that General Dynamics billed the Pentagon $155 for the boarding of an executive's dog, a pooch named Fursten. GD has been snagged for giving a gift of jewelry to the wife of Admiral Hyman Rickover while chalking up $739 million in cost overruns on Rickover's pet project, nuclear submarines. The company has billed the government for substantial amounts in lobbying costs—money spent on efforts to allow GD to make *more* money from the government. In all, the goings-on have been so unsavory as to leave one Congressman "nauseated," to have caused the threatened debarment of top GD execs from continued military contracting, and to have caused chairman David Lewis to announce that he would retire at the end of 1985.

The stepping-down of GD's boss, however, is only a symbolic act, a case of a routed general falling on a rubber sword. The company's ethical problems run far deeper. John F. Lehman, Jr., the Secretary of the Navy, has accused GD of "a pervasive corporate attitude . . . inappropriate to the public trust." The company's main whistleblower, P. Takis Veliotis, is himself holed up in Greece, on the lam from federal kickback charges. And Lester Crown, who has thus far done everything possible to stay behind the scenes, has nevertheless been singled out as a target for outraged public officials. One Congressman, referring to Crown's involvement in the Material Service bribery affair, has accused him of "moral turpitude" and questioned the wisdom of having allowed him on GD's board and given him high-level security clearance in the first place. Another Congressman has simply called him "a crook."

Crown, for his part, has been majestically unflappable. At the height of what will almost certainly stand as one of the late twentieth century's greatest business scandals, he breezily informed *The New York Times* that "there isn't a cultural, ethical change required in this company." Speaking of the charges that have been made against himself in particular, he says that "the worst part of being accused of breaking the law is that in fact our family had grown up being taught moral and ethical values on a plane far higher than anything the law required."

With such lofty standards being inculcated in the home, it clearly would have been redundant and presumptuous for places like the Harvard Business School to imagine there was anything left to teach on the subject of fitting business morality.

"So OK," says Roger Sonnabend, "all of a sudden there's a lot of talk about business ethics, and I think that's great. For all the talk, though, I still don't hear business leaders talking about the really tough issues. It doesn't take a great act of personal courage to go on the record as being against greenmail, against deceptive ads, against foreign bribes.

"But how about the issues where an acceptable stand hasn't yet been defined? How about the things that haven't already been talked into the ground, and that have enormous implications for the future? I don't hear business asking, for example, if it's ethical for the oil companies to be retaining these huge profits, supposedly justified by the need for new explorations, then using the money to scarf up other companies instead. I don't hear business leaders asking whether it's ethical for GM, which is always talking piously about safeguarding American jobs, to be siphoning off resources to diversify into banking or communications. They're hedging their bets for the sake of management and shareholders, which is fine. But what about the workers who don't have that sort of mobility? The company is essentially selling them down the river by now doing everything in its power to strengthen its existing business.

"It's issues like *that* that really get to the guts of contemporary business's ethical dilemmas," Sonnabend maintains. "But when you start raising questions that are subtler than indictable offenses, business people still tend to waffle. They're just not comfortable with the gray zones. And when you bring up issues that cost money, the business community isn't so eager to talk about ethics anymore."

From John Matthews' vantage point at Harvard, the problem stacks up somewhat differently. He can get people to talk about any issue whatsoever, and was doing so decades before the recent vogue for such discussions; talking, after all, is what the academy is for, and getting a spirited exchange cranked up in the classroom is a knack he mastered long ago. For him, the agonizing and perennial question is whether the talking does any good.

Over the course of Matthews' tenure at the Business School, the context of American enterprise has dissolved from a mood of considerable if unspoken solidarity to what sociologist Christopher Lasch has termed "the battle of all against all." The theme of common purpose no longer cuts it, a new rallying cry has yet to take its place, and the upshot in business, ethical chic notwithstanding, has been "an era of 'me-first' management" in which "not just shareholders . . . but corporations themselves, the economy, and even the public at large" are being "let down by a deterioration in ethical behavior in business and on Wall Street."* By 1985, even as the self-appointed business moralists continued holding forth, the *Times* was reporting "a corporate crime wave,"† and produced a poll which indicated that less than one third of all Americans believed corporate executives to be honest. Fifty-nine percent of those surveyed believed that white-collar crime went on "very often," 68 percent felt the government wasn't trying hard enough to stop it, and 65 percent opined that corporate miscreants got off too easy on those rare occasions when they were called to account.‡

For John Matthews, even more than for the rest of us, those statistics constitute some pretty dreary news. If HBS is a boot camp for America's corporate leaders, then Matthews' role there would seem to be that of the anguished chaplain who preaches the need for decency even

---

* "The Era of 'Me-First' Management," *The New York Times*, August 19, 1984, Business Section, p. 1.

† "White-Collar Crime: Booming Again," ibid., June 9, 1985, Business Section, p. 1.

‡ "Low Marks for Executive Honesty," ibid.

in warfare, knowing in his heart that out there in the steam and stench of the jungle his boys will go right on cutting off dead enemies' ears. That role is an honorable but unenviable one, and, all claims and publicity to the contrary aside, it keeps John Matthews and the study of ethics on the fringes of what the Business School is really all about.

Still, John Matthews is not despairing about the teaching or the practice of business ethics, and in fact is heartened by the attitudes he sees in those midcareer executives he deals with in the Advanced Management Program. "These are people," he says, "who already have the job titles and the salaries, who've put the phase of blind ambition behind them, and are now ready to think in terms of what it all adds up to, what the *totality* of a meaningful career in business should include.

"What I tell them is that it has to do with what you want carved into your gravestone. If you're content with the epitaph 'He Pleased His Stockholders,' then you really don't have to do anything except turn a profit and stay within the letter if not the spirit of the law.

"But if that eulogy strikes you as a little paltry, then you've got to do more than that. Convincing people that there *is* more, and that it can be done in ways that are absolutely consistent with the purely pragmatic side of business—that's the challenge, and to this day I still feel the excitement of it every time I set foot in the classroom."

eleven

They're Puppies,
These Yuppies

In 1983, a decidedly bearish year in America, the going
rate for freshly minted Harvard MBAs was hovering between $35,000 and $40,000 a year, or roughly two and a
half times what the '49ers got, even allowing for inflation.
The typical second-year student was being made nice to by
fifteen corporate interviewers. Recruiters who'd run out
the salary offers to the limits of their authority resorted to
sweetening the kitty with fringes like a $5,000 "image
bonus" for picking up togs at Brooks Brothers. Banks
threw parties for the imminent grads, ad agencies took
them to tennis matches, investment houses chartered
yachts to show them Wall Street from the water. Amidst all
this courting of the season's business debutantes, everybody was wondering if the previous year's record high sal-

ary offer would be topped: a 1982 graduate had sashayed out of Soldiers Field into an entry-level slot that paid him a slightly ludicrous $85,000 per annum.

All of this was entertaining enough, but none of it was particularly logical. Demand for new MBAs should have been falling off. By 1983 there were already so many of them glutting the ranks that you couldn't spit in a gentrified neighborhood without hitting one on the leg. Moreover, through the later years of the comeuppance, the MBA mystique had been taking its lumps. MBAs had been assailed for their obsessive reliance on the numbers, for their lack of institutional loyalty and their salacious eagerness for personal advancement, for their overconcentration on short-term goals and their failure as communicators—in short, for playing no small part in getting the American economy into the pickle it was in. Yet American corporations went right on falling all over each other to hire MBAs. Maybe they had no choice. Maybe the game of business had become so thoroughly pigeonholed, so rarefied, so removed from ordinary common sense and skills, that they *had* to stick with the specialists. Still, it was a little odd to assume that a larger dose of the medicine that had made you sick was suddenly going to make you well.

But if the MBA degree no longer implied the infallible business wisdom that it seemed to guarantee in 1949, MBAs themselves were more in fashion than they had ever been. People weren't just talking business now, they were talking life style. Money and the pursuit of same were sweeping back into vogue, and those whose educations had been geared most specifically toward the accumulation of dollars were at the vanguard of the trend. A 1981 *Time* cover story entitled "The Money Chase,"* limned the epic awakening of the baby-boom generation to the hard facts of fiscal adulthood, and paid MBAs the left-handed compliment of describing them, in comparison to their non-MBA coevals, as "chameleons that have mysteriously evolved into some slightly more agile species of lizard."

By 1982, MBAs had become a hot enough item, media-wise, so that two recent HBS grads saw fit to write *The Official M.B.A. Handbook*—a volume that hit the best-seller lists in spite of its inability to decide if its purpose was to summarize, satirize, or glamorize. In fact, the *Handbook* seemed gripped by the same love-hate conflict that the entire culture felt toward the mega-educated business specialists. It observed that there was "no B.S. like H.B.S.," that a Harvard MBA was "often wrong but seldom in doubt," and suggested that what MBA really stood for was "Master of Blind Ambition"; at the same time, the volume promised to make its readers just *like* Harvard MBAs while saving them the trouble and expense of actually going to the school.

In 1983 the term "Yuppie"—for Young Urban Professional—was coined, and it wasn't long before that species, too, had a handbook of its very own. *The Official Yuppie Handbook,* published in 1984, captured both the male and female specimens in amber, with their dual addictions to the *Wall Street Journal* and the Sony Walkman, their fetishes for fresh pasta and spring-loaded running shoes, their entrepreneurial sidelines, their co-op boards, and

---

* *Time,* May 4, 1981, p. 69.

their Solomonic perspicacity in deciding when or if they'd start their families.

Almost overnight the Yuppies became the trendiest and most readily identifiable new class in America, and what it meant was that the neo-eager-beaver ethos was really socking in. Suddenly it was respectable and even perversely hip to work on weekends and to substitute networking for a social life, to wean the libido from carnal desires and direct it instead toward the wooing of wealth. That was the Yuppie way, and Yuppies were suddenly everybody's target audience, role models for everyone who didn't hate their guts, as well as for many people who did. The Yuppies were setting the style and defining the tone, and MBAs from Harvard were cozily ensconced at the very pinnacle of their numbers. Nerds no more, boy MBAs could be proud of their wing-tip shoes, their thin socks, their lugubrious suits and undertakers' overcoats; girl MBAs could slip into a gabardine suit and one of those floppy flaccid bow ties and feel, if not exactly alluring, at least not like a total skank.The MBA style had come to seem so presentable, so *cute*, that in 1985 there was a pinup calendar featuring photos of a dozen eligible bache lors from the Harvard Business School, and *GQ* magazine, in its '85 roundup of America's most desirable women, prominently featured Harvard MBAs among its listings.

If the overweaning ambition of the day was the elegantly simple wish to have it all, these recent veterans of Soldiers Field seemed to be coming about as close as anybody could. With their swollen incomes and financial savvy, they were already able to afford the VCR, the BMW, the IRA, and most of the other letters in the alphabet of affluence. They dined on shiitake mushrooms and routinely traded up on real estate. They had the cowed respect of headwaiters and the envy of their peers. They relished the pivotal roles they were destined to play in an America that was coming back, and they took pride in themselves for having turned out, after long and wacky adolescences, to be just the sort of grownups their elders had prayed that they would be.

There were only two small crimps in the idyll:

Crimp number one was that most of the evidence indicated that America, unfortunately, wasn't coming back. Crimp number two was that many of the new MBAs' better-informed elders—as represented, for example, by the men of '49—were less impressed with the young hotshots than the young hotshots would have liked to think.

"You can't kid a kidder," says Ned Dewey, "and no one is less easily snowed by a Harvard MBA than another Harvard MBA. These kids are smart—you've got to give them that. But in my business I'd as soon take a python to bed with me as hire one. He'd suck my brains, memorize my Rolodex, and use my telephone to find some other guy who'd pay him twice the money."

"Can you tell me," asks '49er William Eiseman, a senior vice-president at Morgan Guaranty bank, "that the average Business School graduate is worth fifteen grand a year more, to start, than someone coming out of, say, Yale without an MBA? I'd say that's ridiculous."

"The problem," observes Jim Burke, who's actually been quizzed by the B School about J&J's long-standing aversion to its grads, "begins with the selection process. If you lean heavily on test scores, you necessarily end up with people who are very adept at quantification. And human nature being what it is, people who are very good at numbers tend to put a lot of faith in numbers. Which means that kids are coming out of business school with less and less language skills, less and less people skills, and more and more to unlearn. The really important decisions don't have anything to do with quantification, as everyone figures out—eventually.''

So go the reservations, and they were being voiced in a context in which, the Yuppie hype notwithstanding, the overall expectations of the baby-boom generation were actually on the skids. Between 1979 and 1983 the median real income of Americans between the ages of twenty-five and thirty-four declined by 14 percent. True, that statistic included a lot of poor slobs who'd been laid off at car factories or textile mills. But not even MBAs were finding themselves immune to the pinch. True, their starting salaries had reached an all-time high; it was also true, however, that they were virtually certain to run into leadership logjams faster than any group that had gone before. Their parents' generation had created far more offspring than new slots in the upper reaches of mainstream business.

By the middle 1980s there were more than half a million active MBAs straining upward in the American workplace. Every year a higher proportion of them were finding themselves bottlenecked at positions like account exec or junior trader, trying to see over the heads of the guys in front of them for a glimpse of the eventual big job. Every June sixty thousand new recruits joined the ranks of MBAs, and they had still *more* heads lined up in front of them. In all, it was a discouraging scenario, and at least some of the foibles ascribed to recent MBAs can be explained largely in terms of simple Darwinian pressures. If the new MBAs were notorious for irresponsible job-hopping, it was at least partly because advancement within a given company was likely to be sluggish. If they were short on loyalty to their firms, it was at least largely because most of the firms they were dealing with could offer them only limited security in return. The widespread perception that the younger MBAs were geared toward nothing but their own success could be seen as largely a response to the fact that now, more than ever, it was a jungle out there.

Largely, but not entirely. This was still the Me Generation, after all, and, as *Newsweek* observed in "The Year of the Yuppie," the cover story of its final issue of 1984, "a generation once notorious for discovering new ways to make itself feel good [was finding] the habit hard to break." The endorphins released by a sprint on the fast track, it was discovered, produced a euphoria not so very different from that previously achieved by transcendental meditation, a midnight plunge in the Pacific, and/or a good hearty whiff of amyl nitrate. It was still a private euphoria. The pursuit of it made people similar while keeping them separate. Business, like life in general, was seen increasingly as an individual sport. And the Yuppies' elder colleagues—even while acknowledging that, by many criteria, the kids were doing awesomely well—reserved the right to disapprove.

Psychoanalyst Abraham Zaleznik, who has studied and taught at the Business School since 1947, observes that "you can infer a lot about the students here, or anywhere, just from the changes that have occurred in the vocabulary of psychology. Back in the forties, nobody talked about an 'identity crisis.' People weren't that self-involved. You didn't worry about identity; you worried about how you functioned in the world—*with* the world. The key word was adjustment."

By the seventies, however, the emphasis had shifted away from the classical neuroses toward a former *rara avis*, the narcissist. "This was really a new wrinkle," says Zaleznik, "a generation of people who were less interested in adjusting than in seeing their own image reflected. Put in MBA terms, they were the careerists. They appeared purposeful and hard-driving—as students here have *always* appeared—but they were calculators, maneuverers. Some sense of belongingness, of shared purpose, had disappeared along the line."

More than anything else, it is this issue of shared purpose that defines the differences between the men of '49 and the MBAs of the late seventies and eighties, and that animates the conflict in their approaches. It's a conflict that happens to run much deeper than management style or career development, because the '49ers aren't just the professional precursors of the Yuppies; they happen to be their parents. The men of '49 have sent an estimated four hundred sons and daughters to HBS, around three hundred to other top-tier business schools around the country, and roughly five hundred to law school. The character of those young men and women, and the business and professional milieu in which they operate, represent the convergence of the '49ers' private and public careers, their successes and their failures in both the grandest and the most intimate arenas. The baby banker computing his way through the arcana of mergers and acquisitions while jobs and companies disappear; the mercurial broker doing brilliantly at her fourth job in three years, while left-behind employers and clients dig out from under; the financial guy who was happiest as a kid when he was tinkering, but got sophisticated enough to know that making things is not the way to go—all of these, whether they realize it or not, are engaged in acting out aspects of the '49ers' legacy.

The Yuppies hold the mirror, and what they reflect is sometimes unsettling to the men of the postwar. Not that the '49ers are necessarily any more objective than other parents about the exploits of their children. Still, one hears occasional notes of wistfulness about what became of the boy with the shiny bike and the brand-new baseball mitt, the girl who cried if you wouldn't let her wear her patent-leather Easter shoes home from the store in the rain.

"Of *course* we spoiled our kids," says one '49er, father of four, two of whom have become MBAs. "Especially for those of us who hadn't grown up with much ourselves, it was one of the great pleasures of life. To send 'em to good schools, give 'em tennis lessons, fiddle lessons—that was part of what was sweet about success. And let's face it—some of it was guilt. Talk to a hundred successful guys my age, and ninety-five of them, if they're being honest, will say they stinted in their attention to their families, that they worked too much and were around too little, that they found it easier to fork over money than to make it home in time for dinner.

"So maybe we showed our kids too much of the fruits of work and too little of the guts of it, too little of the why of it. We tried, but it doesn't seem we did enough. Maybe we went about it wrong. Like, when my boys were teenagers, I used to make them supplement their allowances by caddying at the country club. What I hoped, I guess, was that the experience would put them on terms with physical work—work where you felt it in your legs at the end of the day and someone told you what to do—and I hoped it would give them some compassion for the people whose whole lives would consist of things like that. The Army did that for me, and I wanted *something* to do it for them. I wanted them to realize they were lucky.

"Not long ago I was talking with the younger boy, and I asked him what he thought about when he was dragging golf bags around the course. He told me he tried not to think of anything, and just looked forward to the day when people would be carrying clubs for *him*. I started to tell him that wasn't the point at all, then I stopped. What could I say to him at this point? He's twenty-nine, he's got a terrific job, he just put a down payment on a condo. His way works fine for him, and who am I to tell him that I think maybe something's missing from his view of things? So I figured I'd keep my antique opinions to myself."

Whether the postwar version of common purpose and national mission has in fact become antique is open to discussion. What is clear, however, is that Yuppie assumptions on such matters have evolved in accordance with an economic curve of a very different shape from that which pertained in the years of the long honeymoon. For the generation that came before, the Depression and the war, paradoxically, turned out to be kindnesses. The Depression ended, the war was won, and the victory catapulted America into an era that was more affluent and self-esteeming than anyone would have dared predict. The baby-boomers, on the other hand, came of age believing

that everything was hunky-dory and in addition to the normal anguish of becoming grownups, have had to absorb
the realization that things aren't as hunky-dory as they
used to be. They'd cruised through childhood *knowing*
that next year's car would be bigger than this year's, that
next year's Christmas tree would be a little taller. Like
Alice, they inhabited a world where everything was mysteriously but reliably growing; then, just when they'd finally gotten used to it, just when they were about to have
their turn at *running* it, things just as inexorably started
threatening to shrink. It was so confusing, so heartbreak-
ing really, that it was easier not to try to make sense of it,
but just to change one's posture to fit the new surround-
ings. The alteration was subtle but definite. Whereas the
postwar striving had consisted of an almost Gothic up-
ward-craning of the neck toward the lucent ideal of the
American carrot, the Yuppies' exertions were aimed at
keeping their backsides ahead of the pack, to avoid being
pummeled by the deflationary stick.

At its most flagrant, the new challenge was expressed
in the title of a book by the Reverend Terry Cole-Whit-
taker, pastor of the so-called Yuppie church in San Diego:
How to Have More in a Have-Not World. Putting the matter a shade less odiously, the fact was that personal success became an ever more compelling goal as there came
to be less and less to feel good about *outside* of personal
success. By the mid-eighties it had become an utter com-
monplace that the federal deficit was killing us, that our
former industrial base had had it, and that Social Security
as well as many corporate pension funds would probably
be belly-up by the time the Yuppies' golden hair had
turned to silver. The only sane course seemed to be to keep

the endorphins flowing and salt some bucks away in the meantime.

It was an outlook that justified and even glorified the most unfettered pursuit of personal advantage, yet it implied, as well, a particularly harsh and unyielding sort of pressure. If one's own success, in monetary terms, was the measure of all things, then what if one's own success fell short? Where else was there to turn for gratification? "Harvard [Business School]," observed Geoffrey C. Hazard, then dean of Yale's School of Organization and Management, in 1981, "points with pride to the fact that one of eight of its graduates is a C.E.O. . . . Does that mean that seven out of eight are failures?"

"I worry about these kids," says Connie Jones, who over the years has played mentor to some of the brainiest of them. "They seem to be constantly wrestling with a conflict that I'm not even sure they're aware of: obviously, they're part of the system, yet at the same time they seem to feel that making it means *beating* the system. I don't think we saw it that way. If anything, we erred on the other side—we were going to tie our star to the system and let the system carry us along.

"Maybe that wasn't the best attitude either," he continues, "but I think it made life easier. Sure, we were ambitious as hell. We wanted the big office and the fancy title just like these kids do. But it wasn't like we had to have it or couldn't face ourselves shaving in the morning. It was OK just to have a responsible position with a respected firm, doing something you could feel was other than trivial. It was OK to be a *part* of something. The young comers today—it's not that they're cynical, exactly. That's the easy answer, but I don't think it's anything that conscious.

They're lonely, is what I think it comes down to. And if you're lonely to begin with, you feel like you may as well be lonely at the top.

"As long as these kids are on the move, they're fine. But I'm concerned about what'll happen to them when they stall in their meteoric rises—as of course the great majority of them will. As the great majority of *every* class does, including ours. When the newness wears off and they have to sit still long enough to look inside themselves, I'm not sure what they'll make of what they find."

Not that the MBAs of recent years are all *that* different from the men of '49.

True, in certain substantive matters the dissimilarities are striking and profound. The rise of consulting and the still increasing draw of Wall Street; the burgeoning popularity of Finance at the expense of Manufacturing and Marketing; the almost nomadic mobility that now pertains among the whiz kids—these changes are so basic as almost to constitute a redefinition of what the MBA degree is all about, of the species of competence it seeks to confer; the implications of those shifts will be examined for many years to come.

In other ways, however, the case can be made that the essential *modus operandi* of the MBA hasn't changed at all—that it has always consisted, and consists still, of the most singleminded and efficient motion toward the juiciest possible niche in whatever version of business happens to be most in fashion at the time. Business doesn't call it fashion, of course, and it doesn't feel like fashion to those immersed in it. To today's MBA, a terminal and a telephone at Goldman, Sachs or at McKinsey feels like destiny, just as cutting one's teeth at P&G or Westinghouse had been kismet for the men of the Organization days. The game, unquestionably, has been rewritten, but it can be argued that the players haven't really changed.

"You know," says John Grant, "one of the annoying but also poignant things about these whippersnappers is that they all fancy themselves as high-blown strategists, they all want to play corporate planner. Two years of case method, and they all think they're ready to fly the airplane.

"But I'll let you in on a little secret: we weren't any different. We wanted to play the big game, too. The only difference was that *we* could get away with it, we had a wide open field to romp around in. Today . . . Look, how many good, exciting, *thinking* jobs are there at most companies? Maybe four. Maybe six. Everybody wants 'em, but the hard and simple fact is that just about all those chairs are filled."

Grant pauses, looks out his high window at the skyline, then surveys his big office with a mixture of satisfaction and sheepishness.

"And more than a few of them," he resumes, "are still filled by *us*. I mean, sorry, kids, but there it is."

Conclusion

The Last American Optimists

Bill Eiseman, a senior officer at one of America's biggest banks, still thinks fifty dollars is a lot of money.

"It's crazy," he says. "All day long we deal in millions, billions, but to this day, when I look down and see a fifty-dollar bill in my own wallet, I feel this instant of boyish excitement, I almost want to fold it up and put it in my shoe. I can remember when fifty dollars was a month's wages. I remember when having that much cash at once qualified you as a wealthy man."

Roger Sonnabend remembers reaching up to hold his father's hand while crossing slushy Boston streets on winter weekends, going to collect rent on the residential buildings that the elder Sonnabend owned. "We'd visit maybe twenty tenants," recalls the son, "and if four of them had rent to give us, we considered it a successful morning. Six out of twenty, we celebrated. In those years, causes for celebration were decidedly relative."

Causes for optimism were equally so; yet optimism, in hard-knocks America of the thirties and the forties, simmered, seethed, and eventually spilled over in a torrent of hot bubbles. The Depression probably wouldn't last forever, and that was a reason to be optimistic. The war would probably end soon, and probably the other side would lose, and those were reasons to be optimistic. The spurts and stalls of the immediate postwar economy—chances were they'd get ironed out before the Stock Exchange caved in again, so why not be optimistic about that? This was optimism with a grain of sheer splendid lunatic defiance in it. It was optimism that started from the bottom, that brooked no contrary evidence, and that shaped perceptions like an iron pan around a wad of rising dough. It was the cheeky, provincial, shrill, and sublime optimism of a people just being smitten by the realization that the moment of its world-beating greatness was at hand.

The men of Harvard B School, '49, possessed that optimism, or were possessed by it, in spades. From their lookout at Soldiers Field, they saw lush perspectives of America's potential and their own, as snugly interwoven as the strands of a Seminole basket. Their graduation year would be the centennial of that *other* gold rush, and the Class of '49 took the coincidence to heart. They adopted as their logo a little hand-drawn prospector, a digger with a pick and shovel stashed in an HBS rucksack slung over his shoulder. He's not a glamorous figure, nor a heroic one. But he's nobody's fool and, most of all, he's ready. Plodding on, leaning forward, his face midway between a grin and a determined grimace, he gives off the insular cheer-fulness that goes with fanatical certainty. He knows where the gold is, that prospector does. He knows he'll be able to claw it out of the ground. And he knows that the particular quest he's undertaken is the fitting thing for a man to do.

He knows that because in 1949 business was more than an amalgam of individual careers, more than a mo-saic of individual ambitions. Enterprise, in its earnest if convenient estimation of itself, was a shared crusade, fit-ted with a rhetoric as pompous and inflaming as that which launches holy wars, or cold ones. "I say to you as emphatically as I can," wrote HBS Marketing Professor Malcolm McNair in the "Faculty Opinion" column of the Spring 1949 *Alumni Bulletin,* "that our social salvation and the preservation of our liberties depend in no small degree on business . . . keeping itself strong, vigorous, and healthy."

But if the stakes were monumental, the faith that the game could in fact be won was made of granite. "Some-thing Is Happening in America," breathed the title of an-other 1949 "Faculty Opinion," this one penned by James Culliton, the man who instilled the '49ers with PR&R. That something was a "reaffirmation of our belief in spir-itual values" and a heightened conviction that those values constituted "the most potent force in the continued developmen. of America and the dynamic preservation . . . of Americanism." This was the forties version of being born again, and its expansive, optimistic fervor makes the most recent visitation seem crabbed and desperate. Not that the national economy and the national fate were being left in the hands of mystics. No, the crux of the day's beliefs resided in a simple trust in hard work and Yankee ingenuity, that trust ennobled by the understanding that nuts-and-bolts competence, after all, was a signature aspect of Americans' providential gift.

"Why Is U.S. Industry So Productive?" The question was modestly raised, in the year of the '49ers' Commencement, by Public Policy Professor Sumner Slichter, who then went on to answer it himself. American industry outperformed all others because of a combination of factors that apparently had less to do with technical prowess than with moral superiority; other countries had the same machines, as Slichter pointed out, but couldn't seem to make them go. In America, however, business prospered because of an atmosphere in which person and property were secure, in which ambition was not hamstrung by rigid social strata, in which a privileged and enormous middle class provided a grateful market for almost anything. Finally, America outproduced all other countries because "industry in the United States is largely in the hands of men who desire to make money rather than to enjoy wealth."

This last was a crucial, slightly perverse, and stunningly accurate observation, even as it applied to the still developing tastes and preferences of the Class of '49. They would not, as a group, go in for luxury. They would not be drinkers of old Margaux or avid collectors of notable canvases. They would tend to take vacations only when their long-suffering wives insisted, and then would sit glumly on their balconies, reading the paper and casting disapproving glances at the Grand Canal or the Ionian Sea. They would ride in the obligatory limos, because that was what a corporate president did; they would take the Lear jet for efficiency's sake; they would occasionally smoke the two-dollar cigar because that, after all, had become an icon. Beyond that, they would cleave by and large to a staunch republican austerity, and proudly so.

There was something manly, bracing, and virtuous about accumulating money; there was something effeminate, enervating, Persian about craving the things that money bought. The issue, seldom baldly stated, was decadence, and the men of '49 looked upon it with righteous horror. Unwittingly, first by their very success, then by their legacy of diminished hopes, they would set the stage for decadence in the generation that came after. For themselves, however, they would fend it off to the very end.

Thirty years after graduation, when his total income was in the neighborhood of a million dollars a year, Jim Burke would still agonize over the purchase of a beach-front cottage, something he'd wanted all his life. "Aw, why not go ahead and buy it, Jim?" he'd be coaxed by friend Tom Murphy, the first person in history to acquire a television network. "Guys like you and me are gonna run out of time before we run out of cash."

Besides, what, then, was all that work *about*?

It was, finally, about itself, means and end as thoroughly marbled together as anything ever cooked up in the caldron of Ad Prac. The work led to the money. The money proved you were playing a significant role in the game. But the role was only significant if the game itself was of consequence, so you worked in order that the game itself would prosper. You succeeded in proportion as the game succeeded, praising the game while inventing the game, feeding off of it while doing all you could to make the game glorious. It was the optimism of the big time that held the cycle together. As long as you believed the game was getting grander, richer, more confirmed in its essential rightness, it would be not only mean-spirited but stupid to withdraw your labors, your money, and your hopes from the swelling, spiraling heart of it. You'd be depriving yourself of a share in destiny. Anybody could see that.

The pathos of history does not consist in unpreventable defeats or ineluctable catastrophes. It consists, rather, in things that might have turned out differently had a danger been perceived, had a solution been offered, a decade, a year, a minute sooner; it consists in the haunting awareness of chances missed.

In 1986 the United States is still by usual measures the most prosperous nation in the world. But, relative to the growth of certain other countries as well as to the rate of its own previous expansion, it has been for some years in decline. The U.S. will never again be quite as dominant or quite as cocksure as in the days of the long honeymoon. Its promise is no longer quite so lavish, so beguiling, or so general. And it is precisely those things that America had previously been proudest of, that had made its inspiring and self-renewing optimism palatable to people of conscience, that have taken a beating. The middle class is shrinking. The gap between rich and poor is widening. The next generation is likely to be worse off, not better.

Those are facts. There is nothing to argue about them. For the men of '49, the only argument that still seems to matter is whether things could have turned out otherwise.

The years immediately following World War II had been a lopsided, unnatural, and therefore unstable moment in the ebb and surge of nations. The Soviet Union had lost almost seventy men for every American dead. The factories of England, France, Germany, and Japan had been blown up, sabotaged, or melted. Crops in much of the developed world had been destroyed or gone unharvested. Currencies of defeated regimes were virtually worthless. That was the decimated context in which America rocketed to its preeminence; yet America—like every other championship nation in the history of the world—preferred to overlook the role of circumstance and accident, and to see its rise solely as the inevitable vindication of the national character, the national brains, and the national worthiness.

Not that American dominion wasn't hard-earned. It assuredly was. Still, had less pseudo-patriotic mouthing off been indulged in during the uncontested glory days, there might have been less anguish and less befuddlement once a more reasonable international balance began to reassert itself. And the glory days might have gone on longer. Because, even with this scant degree of hindsight, it seems clear that the profoundest and most damaging mistake made by the postwar generation of American business leaders lay in their refusal or inability to take other countries, especially non-European countries, seriously. "The future," as the *Atlantic* would later observe, "belong[ed] to those who [would] sell to the world," but America, with its vast and flush domestic market and its recent memories of conquered, cashless foreigners, had a tough time conceiving of a world worth selling to. Still less could America imagine being economically invaded by waves of highly desirable foreign goods. Where would they come from? Germany? OK, Germany you had to respect, but it would take them, say, thirty years to come up to speed. Hong Kong? Hong Kong only made counterfeit Swiss watches and cheap sweatshirts that shrank all to hell in the dryer. Japan? Japan turned out fake-leather baseballs that Oriental newspaper came flying out of the first time you gave them a good American wallop. This was competition?

If America's postwar underestimate of foreign resilience was epic, its *over*estimate of its own capacity for progressive change was heroic, poignant, big-hearted, and ultimately embittering. While such catholicity seems wildly distant now, the fact is that before Senator Joe McCarthy had bullied the nation into a hysterical polarity, America had been willing to look soberly at Soviet Russia and to regard that country's socioeconomic system as a legitimate and salutary challenge to its own. You didn't have to *like* socialism, still less Communism, to feel that its promises and appeal were worth addressing, that it spoke to certain human desires that capitalism, too, must seek to satisfy. In 1949 a free-enterpriser with credentials as impeccable as those of Norman Gras, who taught Business History at Soldiers Field, could applaud the dynamic whereby Russia's "implied threat to our way of life [would] hasten our process of socializing from within."

Under the benign aegis of what Gras called "the new business statesmanship," the American system would undo the abuses of classical bareknuckled capitalism and "prove that Karl Marx . . . had not formulated his theory of social processes with sufficient discrimination." America would refute Marx by outdoing him, by taking such splendid care of its working classes—with training, with wages, with benefits, with security—that the idea of proletarian rebellion and even the notion of unionism would come to seem quaint, superfluous, absurd.

It was a boldly openhanded conception, as well as a pragmatic one, and on the upward slope of the big time it more or less seemed to be holding up in practice. American employees drove Buicks, ate steak, bought shares, and retired to Coconut Grove. American managers had the psychic luxury of feeling like benefactors as well as bosses. But at some point the goodwill started seeming too expensive; it also started seeming that a lot of it had been built on fibs.

"Socializing from within" had sounded nice and even somewhat dangerously exciting. But all along, the income differential between workers and top management in the U.S. had been dramatically more pronounced than in Japan, Germany, and nearly every other industrial nation. By the seventies, corporations had begun pressuring unions for wage concessions even as executive compensation packages continually became more lavish. Amid righteous complaints about the lagging productivity of the American worker, corporate raiders and lame-duck boards were passing hundreds of millions of dollars back and forth for producing nothing whatsoever. Companies in mature industries were increasingly choosing simply to buy into sexier fields rather than retrain their employees. The gloves were off again, so far as the primacy of profit was concerned; the various constituencies of American enterprise had seldom been more seethingly at odds. In 1980, in the face of a serious wave of layoffs, a United Steel Workers economist opined that "there is less danger of communism today in Tokyo than in Youngstown." By

1983 only 18 percent of Americans expressed "great confidence" in the country's executives. So much for business statesmanship.

And so much for the age of optimism. That age was entering its death throes around the time of the '49ers' silver jubilee, and by their thirty-fifth reunion, in 1984, the memory of it was already going sepia around the edges. Not that the vocabulary of great expectations had fallen suddenly into disuse. No, like the Goodyear blimp, the rhetoric could still be pumped up and floated fatly by to impart a celebratory air when called for. Politicians still made optimism a keynote. Best-selling books could still be palmed off on the theme. Wall Street still went blue in the face trying to keep the balloon afloat. And of course every Yuppie worth his or her coarse-grained salt cherished the conviction that he or she, at least, would get over in a manner of some flamboyance. But it wasn't quite the same.

"Somewhere along the line," says Ned Dewey, "it got away from us. That feeling that the whole wide world was blossoming. The idea that ambition just naturally had two sides to it—to get something for yourself, but also to do something that mattered. What passes for optimism today—we had a different word for it. We just called it greed, and we didn't mean it as a compliment."

Stanley Greenfield has two dead plants on his windowsill and an industrial-size bottle of aspirin, half empty, on his desk. The floor of his small office is covered in linoleum, and next to an ancient dented file cabinet he has a mini-fridge that holds two vanilla yogurts, half a chicken-salad sandwich, and a bottle of Cremora.

Greenfield works alone now. He'd gone the corporate route for almost thirty years, and seems to have gotten it quite thoroughly out of his system. He's been an ad man, a space salesman, a publisher, the creator of a magazine, and a president of someone else's company. Now at the age of sixty-three, he has the job title consultant and entrepreneur.

As a one-man operation, he's come back to his natural mode. He scuffs around his linoleum floor, pacing laps around his metal desk, popping aspirin till he thinks up an idea. When he has one, he goes scrambling out of his office and running down the hall, stuffing his arms into his jacket as he goes, heading out to find investors. "I'm a salesman," Stanley Greenfield says. "I've always been a salesman."

He lives on Fifth Avenue these days, a base from which it's very easy to keep up with former classmates. John Grant and Wilbur Cowett are just down the way, and then there's Jack Shad from the SEC, who keeps a Manhattan residence on Park, and Connie Jones over by the river. Not that Greenfield, any more than the rest of us, has to go visiting to stay in contact with the Class of '49. Like the rest of us, he can feel their presence just by making copies on one of Pete McColough's Xerox machines or picking out some ties at Marv Traub's Bloomingdale's; he can watch Tom Murphy's television network to keep himself apprised of Lester Crown's submarines and scandals; at the end of the day he can stroll home past what used to be Ernie Henderson's Sheraton Hotel and Roger Sonnabend's Plaza, and can cool his tired toes with Jim Burke's baby powder.

"No one ever said our timing wasn't good," he says.

The hair on his arms is salt-and-pepper, the skin is a little loose around his collar, but his delivery remains emphatic, his vocal range impressive. "But we also had this attitude—we were stubborn, tenacious, we stuck like glue. We were *all* salesmen. You made your pitch, and if you didn't like the response you got, you just rephrased the question. Or you waited. Guy wasn't buying this week, maybe he'd be buying next week. Door was closed today, maybe somebody would open it tomorrow. You know what it was? We were a group that just didn't know how to take no for an answer."

Greenfield pauses. The telephone rings. He reaches for the receiver with one hand and jabs a finger toward the ceiling with the other. "Which doesn't necessarily mean we always asked the smartest questions. But that's another story. What can I tell you? Hang on a minute. Hello?"

index